NONWOVEN REINFORCED COMPOSITES

POOJA KATKAR
PROF. (DR.) P.V.KADOLE
ASHISH HULLE

Textile Academic Publishing

NONWOVEN REINFORCED COMPOSITES

First e-book edition published 2019 in India.
ISBN: 9781794018365

Published by Textile Academic Publishing and Services an imprint of Ashish Hulle
For more copies of this book, please email: books@jtcsonline.com
Tel: +919665854452

Designed and Set by Ashish Hulle
www.jtcsonline.com
Cover design by Ashish Hulle
Illustrations by Ashish Hulle

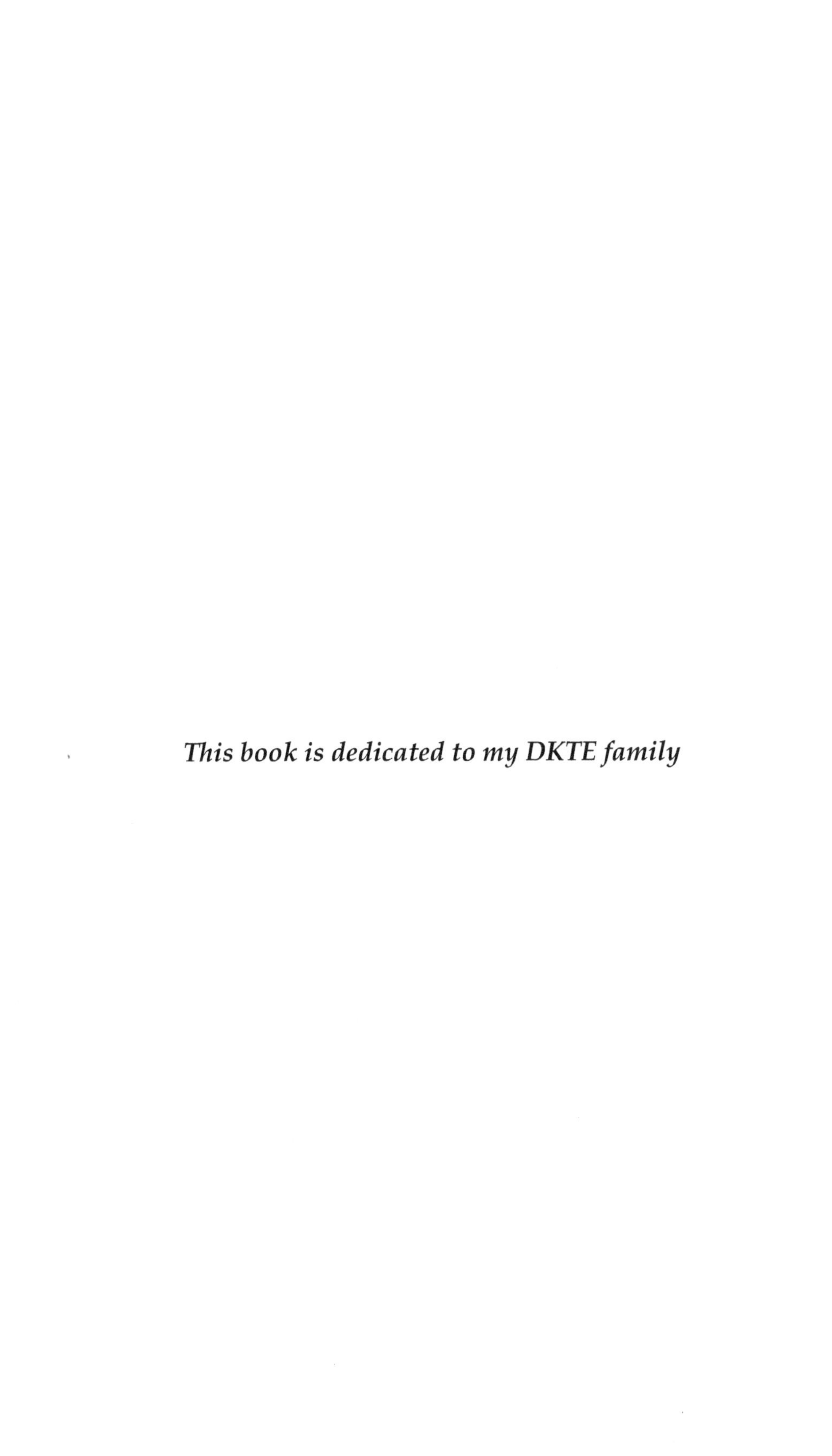

This book is dedicated to my DKTE family

CONTENTS

Nonwoven Reinforced Composites

ACKNOWLEDGEMENT

I would like to express my sincere gratitudes to the following people, who contributed their time to help prepare this book.

- Special thanks to Prof.(Dr.) P. V. Kadole, who has guided me all the time.
- Prof.(Dr.)U. J. Patil, who has given the inspiration to write this book
- All my colleagues and friends who helped and encouraged me
- My family for support.

CHAPTER 1

INTRODUCTION

Innovative, cost-effective and handy materials are the what, today's market demand. Researchers are therefore involved in accomplishing these demands of the market, in turn, industries. A wide spectrum of products, right from the decently decorative to multifaceted, engineered structures, combining properties of different materials into a one, in the form of composite. They may be designed to varieties of end applications as per demands: lustrous or dull, impervious or permeable, thick or thin, plane or moulded, with limits to the sky to its size, virtually. Composites find applications in most of the areas of day-to-day life, viz. roofing, furniture, packing, tanks, pipes, vehicle bodies, buildings, and so on.

To produce a textile reinforced composite structure, two basic components are essential, these being a matrix and a textile fibre. Textile fibres are reinforced in the matrix to form a composite structure, wherein, physical and chemical individualities of both fibres and matrix are retained with the consolidation of properties, which cannot be accomplished with the constituents acting alone. Hence, while fabricating composites, matrix and the reinforced materials should be chosen to empower us to make better use of their merits while curtailing to some extent their deficiencies.

Unlike conventional fixed track processes, in composite manufacturing industries, engineers can rethink about the basic components and find better solutions owing to freedom of selection of appropriate material and method while designing the products, meeting exact needs of consumers. Tougher and lighter materials with tailored properties can be made easily through composite forming technology. Thus, ease of manufacturing complex shapes, freedom to select the constituents and appropriate technique, enables to manufacture composite structures in a more reliable form which can often lead to both cheaper and better solutions.

CHAPTER 2
ABOUT COMPOSITES

Stone Age, the Bronze Age, and the Iron Age, and now its Composite Age.

'Composites' a Latin word, meaning put together signifying something made by putting together different parts or materials [1]. Advances in materials are one of the signs of development of mankind. The present era of material belongs to the several advantages associated with composite materials.

The composites are not new to mankind; it has a history of more than 3000 years. In ancient Egypt, people used to build walls from the bricks made of mud with straw as reinforcing component [2]. Another important application of composites can be seen around 1200 AD from Mongols. Mongolians invented a bow made up of composites. Using a combination of animal glue, bone and wood, bows were pressed and wrapped with birch bark [3].

In the 1960s with the introduction of polymer-based composites, composite starts getting the attention of industries, because of several advantages associated with this structural material, these are lighter weight, higher strength, corrosion resistance, convertibility, durability, etc. Since after, composites have gained a prominent share as a common engineering material in various industries. Increased awareness in terms of performance of the product, the price of the material and increased competition for lightweight components, in the world market is another specific reason for the growth in composite usage [4].

Nowadays there is an increasing demand for the products and manufacturing techniques which are accessible, reproducible and economical. The success of composites in applications is dependent on these factors. Composites can be fabricated even more according to an integrated design process resulting in the optimum construction according to parameters such as shape, mass, strength, stiffness, durability, costs, etc. [5]. Newly developed design tools must be able to instantaneously show customers the influence of a design change on each one of these parameters. Technologist, therefore, should focus on designing the products considering these facts. Thus, in future, composite structure has a huge market since there is tremendous scope for production of these materials using a vast range of combinations of reinforcement and the matrix, to meet consumer's need.

2.1 Definitions of composite [1]

As per the Textile Institute Textile Terms and Definitions, the composite is defined as a product formed by intimately combining two or more discrete physical phases, usually a solid matrix and a fibrous material.

As per the ASTM (Committee D-30 on Composite Materials) standard D3878–07, a composite material is defined as a substance consisting of two or more materials, insoluble in one another, which are combined to form a useful engineering material possessing certain properties not possessed by the constituents. Further, a composite material is inherently inhomogeneous on a microscopic scale, but can often be assumed to be homogeneous on a macroscopic scale for certain engineering applications. The constituents of a composite retain their identities: they do not dissolve or otherwise merge completely into each other, although they act in concert.

As per the dictionary of man-made fibres, composites are materials with plastics as matrix and high tenacity fibres or short fibres as reinforcement; without this reinforcement, plastics would be insufficiently rigid, solid and impact resistant. Thus the man-made fibre industry thinks about composites as fibre-reinforced and plastic- matrix composites only.

The polymer industry however typically follows another definition of the composite. The Encyclopedia of Polymer Science and Technology defines composites as combinations of materials differing in composition or form on a macroscopic scale in which all of the constituents in the composites retain their identities and do not dissolve or otherwise completely merge into each other.

The North American Association of the Nonwoven Fabrics Industry (INDA) and the European Disposables and Nonwovens Association (EDANA) jointly define a composite material as a macroscopic combination of two or more distinct materials, having a recognizable interface between them.

From the above definition, it clearly results that each industry thus follows its own definition of composites. It appears that each of these industries has different circumstances and motivations. So it is no wonder that they have pushed their own criteria for defining composites. What has to be achieved during the design and the fabrication of a composite material, is the incorporation into its structure of a synergic effect so as to be able to obtain "a new material possessing superior properties to the individual components, either alone or mixed together".

2.2 Areas of application

Composite materials have a wide range of applications. They possess applications in buildings and public works (chimneys, housing cells, door panel, windows, partitions, swimming pools, furniture and bathrooms); electrical and electronics (insulation for electrical construction, armor, boxes, covers, cable tracks, antennas, tops of television towers, and wind mills); general mechanical components (gears, bearings, housing, casing, jack body, robot arms, flywheels, weaving machine rods, pipes, components of drawing table, compressed gas bottles, tubes for offshore platforms and pneumatics for radial frames); rail transports (front of power units, wagons, door, seat, interior panels and ventilation housing); road transports (body components, complete body, wheel, shields, radiator grills, transmission shaft, suspension spring, chassis, suspension arms, casing, cabin, seats, highway tankers and isothermal trucks); marine transports (hovercrafts, rescue crafts, patrol boats, trawlers, anti-mine ships, racing boats, pleasure boats and canoes); space transport (nozzles, rocket boosters, reservoirs and shields for atmosphere re-entrance); air transports (all composite passenger aircrafts and gliders, helicopter blades, propellers, transmission shafts and aircraft brake discs); cable transports; sports and recreation (poles used in jumping, tennis and squash rackets, fishing poles, bicycle frames, roller skates, skies, sails, javelins, surf boards, bows and arrows, protection helmets, golf clubs and oars) , etc. [6].

2.3 Classification of composites

Based on the type of reinforcement and matrix, composite materials are classified into two categories.

2.3.1 Classification Based on Matrix [7]

The matrix is the component that holds the filler together to form the bulk material. The matrix in composites is primarily of three types. Based on the matrix, composites are classified into:

a) Polymer matrix composites e.g. Asphalt concrete, Syntactic foam, etc.,

b) Metal matrix composites e.g. White cast iron, Hard metal, etc.,

c) Ceramic matrix composites e.g. Bone, Concrete, etc.

a) Polymer Matrix Composites

Polymers make ideal materials as they can be processed easily, possess lightweight, and desirable mechanical properties. There are two main types of polymers, viz. thermosets and thermoplastics.

Polymers are most suited for advanced conditions of fibre reinforced composite, because of several advantages offered by them. They are flexible, form a well bonded three-dimensional molecular structure after curing, decompose instead of melting on hardening, through small alteration in basic composition suitability towards product can be improved. Thermoset fibre composites find applications in aerospace components, automobile parts, defense systems, etc. Epoxy, polyester, phenolic polyamide resins are commonly used as thermosets resins. The advantages like very easy to manufacture, fast curing and very cheap have made the polyester resin most common in textile reinforced structures [8]. Polyester resin is used to manufacture components in the automotive industry, marine industry, etc. It finds less scope in structural applications, especially, which undergo high temperature. Compare to epoxy and vinyl ester polyester resin shows low tensile strength. Vinyl ester resins are a hybrid form of polyester resin strengthen by addition of epoxy resin. Vinyl ester resins show good resistance toward organic solvents, good impact resistance, and excellent thermal stability. Compare to polyester resin and vinyl ester resin, epoxy is superior because of its basic aromatic structure. Epoxy resin shows excellence in impact resistance, thermal stability, water resistance, etc. so are used in structural applications like components of aircraft.

Thermoplastic resins have one or two-dimensional molecular structure and show the exaggerated melting point. The main advantage of these resins is that the process of softening at elevated temperatures can be reversed. Thermoplastic composites have the major drawback of loss of strength at elevated temperatures. Nevertheless, recompenses in terms of rigidity, toughness and resistance to creep, place them in the important composite materials bracket. They are used in automotive control panels, electronic products encasement, etc. Common kinds of thermoplastics are polyethene, polystyrene, polyamides, nylons, and polypropylene.

b) Metal Matrix Composites

Metals like Titanium, Aluminium, and Magnesium and alloys

are used as matrices with non-reactive reinforcement, stable over a range of temperature. These composites are characterized by high strength, fracture toughness and stiffness. They are particularly useful for aircraft applications.

c) Ceramic Matrix Composites

Ceramics exhibit very strong ionic bonding in general and few cases of covalent bonding, suitable for high-temperature applications above 1500^0C. High melting points, good corrosion resistance, stability at elevated temperatures and high compressive strength, are few advantages of ceramic-based composites. To compensate low tensile strength of ceramic, a material like fibre is reinforced fibre to increase load-bearing capacity.

2.3.2 Classification Based on Reinforcements [9]

The main function of reinforcing constituents in composites provide the strength to the composite. Reinforcement in the composite can be of three different types, so based on reinforcement composites are classified into:

a) Fibre Reinforced composites: e.g. Wood, Glass-fibre reinforced plastic, etc.
b) Laminar composites: e.g. Arborite. Formica (plastic), etc.
c) Particulate composites: e.g. reinforced rubber, concrete, etc.

Fibre Reinforced composites can be further divided into those containing discontinuous or continuous fibres. Laminar Composites are composed of layers of materials held together by the matrix. Sandwich structures fall under this category. Particulate Composites are composed of particles distributed or embedded in a matrix body. The particles may be flakes or in powder form.

a) Fibre Reinforced Composites

In fibre reinforced composites, fibres (natural or synthetic) are used as reinforcing materials in different forms and architectures. Textile composite is a kind of fibre reinforced composites, where textile fibres are used as reinforcing the material. The fibre element performs the main load-bearing component in fibre reinforced composites; length, shape, orientation, and composition of the fibres decide the performance. These types of composites create lightweight yet durable and rigid materials. Fibre reinforced composites can be classified according to the form in which the reinforcement fibre material is used. The orientation of the fibre in the matrix is an indication of the strength of the composite, so the direction of fibres is decided considering the direction of load application. Organic and inorganic fibres are used to reinforce composite materials. Almost all organic fibres have low density, flexibility, and elasticity while inorganic fibres possess high modulus, high thermal stability and greater rigidity than organic fibres. It goes without saying that fibre composites may be constructed with either continuous or short fibres. They can be further classified according to the structure of the reinforcement such as woven, nonwoven, braided, knitted, etc.

b) Laminar composites

To achieve a certain thickness of the product composites are formed, using several layers in the prepreg. These composites, comprising layers of materials held together by the matrix, are considered as multi-layer or laminate composites. Several combinations of laminates account for, metal-metal laminates metal-plastic laminates, vinyl-metal laminates, organic films-metals laminates. Laminates can also be composed of reinforcement as textile structures like layers of nonwoven, woven fabrics, braided fabrics, fibre mats, etc.

c) Particulate Reinforced Composites

Microstructures of metal and ceramics composites, which show particles of one phase strewn in the other, are known as particle reinforced composites. Reinforced particles may have different shapes such as square, triangular and round. The dimensions of all sides of these particles are observed to be more or less equal. The diameter of the particles, the inter-particle spacing, and the volume fraction of the reinforcement, along with matrix properties influence the performance of the particulate reinforced composite.

CHAPTER 3
TEXTILE REINFORCED COMPOSITES

Textile reinforced composites are fibre reinforced composites whose unit reinforcement structures are characterized by more than one fibre orientation. The unit cells are formed through textile processes that manipulate either individual fibres or yarn bundles to create an integral structure. These materials are typically formed from hierarchical systems built from fibres, yarns, and fabric structures [10]. Textile-reinforced composites comprise of various forms of fibres, viz. short fibre, filament woven fabrics, knitted fabrics, stitched fabrics, braids, nonwovens, and multi-axial fabrics, etc., reinforced into polymeric matrix [11]. With this huge range of textile structures, they offer enormous potential for development varieties of composites, since these textile reinforcements have their own characteristic features, which gets translated into the composite, which is a driving force for growing interest from both the academic community and from industry in this area. Textile reinforcements viz. fibres, yarn and most products derived from them, when combined with a binding matrix, usually polymeric, are called as textile reinforced composites. To provide integrity and strength to the structure by carrying the majority of the applied structural loads is the drive of fibre as reinforcement. Most of the fibres have to rupture before the complete failure of the composite and hence usually warning signs are there before the collapse. Textile reinforced composites are used for load-bearing applications in a number of industrial applications. Because of cost-effectiveness, ease of manufacture and performance spectra textile reinforced composites, proposals substantial prospects for new applications. Although the reasons for adopting a particular material can be various and complex, the primary cause for the use of textile reinforcements is undoubtedly cost. Textiles is a flexible, versatile and mass production system with reasonable cost, adopting modern, automated manufacturing techniques. Textiles as, reinforcing material offer the means of forming a composite structure of high strength and stiffness, combined with low density, while the matrix transfer stresses between the fibres, provide a barrier against an adverse environment and protect the surface of fibres from mechanical abrasion.

The modern use of fibre-reinforced polymer composites began in the years near World War II, using glass fibres. The Chevrolet Corvette of 1950 had a fibreglass body [12]. Aerospace, packing, marine, military and defense, automotive, construction, wind turbines, consumer product industries, sports goods, etc. are some target areas of textile reinforced composite [13].

3.1 Factors affecting textile reinforced composite

Pickering et al. reviewed factors critically influencing the mechanical properties of composites. Those are fibre and matrix selection, interfacial strength, fibre dispersion and orientation, porosity and manufacturing processes [14].

3.1.1 Fibre and matrix selection

Good compatibility between the fibre and the matrix is a key challenge to achieve. For optimal mechanical performance, fibres with higher strength are preferred. Regarding the matrix selection, also multiple considerations are required. From a technical point of view, the polymer selected has to fulfil the mechanical and other functional requirements for the application, as well as being suitable for the production process defined. The matrix requires performing an optimal stress transfer in order to achieve a composite with good mechanical performance There are possibilities of matrix modification or fibre treatment that can enhance this interaction is required. Other factors to be taken into account in the matrix selection lie in the fact that it provides protection to the fibres, since acts as a barrier against adverse environments.

3.1.2 Fibre/matrix interaction

When the fibres and matrix selected present a weak interface, the stress-transfer is affected, leading to a poor reinforcement effect of the fibres that can, in extreme cases, ever deteriorate the performance of the bare matrix due to the introduction of small defects that act as stress concentrators. Nowadays there are numerous possibilities for increasing such compatibility between the fibre and the matrix. Concerning the fibre modification, there are many treatments of physical, chemical or enzymatic nature that can be applied in order to adapt the fibre surface for an enhancement of the strength of the composite.

3.1.3 Fibre content and porosity

The fibre content in the composite is expressed in terms of fibre volume fraction or/and fibre weight fraction [15].

Volume Fractions

The volume of the composite material is equal to the sum of the volume of the fibres and the volume of the matrix.

Therefore,

$$V_f + V_m = 1,$$

Where,

- V_f = Volume fraction of fibre (Volume of fibre / Volume of composite)
- V_m = Volume fraction of matrix (Volume of matrix/ Volume of composite)

Weight Fractions

The weight of the composite material is equal to the sum of the weight of the fibres and the weight of the matrix.

Therefore,

$$W_f + W_m = 1,$$

Where,

- W_f = Volume fraction of fibre (Weight of fibre/ Weight of composite)

- W_m = Volume fraction of matrix (Weight of matrix/ Weight of composite)

Density

The density of composite, ρ_{ct} the material can be defined as the ratio of the weight of the composite material to the volume of the composite material and is expressed as

$$\rho_{ct} = \frac{1}{\dfrac{Wf}{\rho f} + \dfrac{Wm}{\rho m}}$$

Actual density, ρ_{ac} of the composites, was determined by measuring weight and the volume of the composite sample.

Void Content

During the incorporation of fibres into the matrix or during the manufacturing of laminates, air or other volatiles may be trapped in the material. The trapped air or volatiles exist in the laminate as micro voids, which may significantly affect some of its mechanical properties. A high void content usually leads to lower fatigue resistance, greater susceptibility to water diffusion, and increased variation (scatter) in mechanical properties. The void content V_v, in a composite, can be estimated by comparing the theoretical density with its actual density.

$$V_v = \frac{\rho_{ct} - \rho_{ac}}{\rho_{ct}}$$

The increase in fibre content is generally translated into a rise in the mechanical properties of the composite. A higher amount of fibres will be translated into higher stiffness and in higher composite strength. ratio. The porosity has an important effect in lowering the final properties of the composite. The orientation of the fibres with respect to the direction in which the load is applied plays a key role. However, fibre orientation can be a positive or negative factor depending on the processing technique and final application of the composite. Regarding the fibre dispersion, it is an extremely important factor since a random and good distribution of the fibres has to be achieved to produce isotropic material, in which the fibres are fully surrounded by the matrix, not agglomerated, to reach a good stress-transfer. The increase in the length of the fibres eases their trend to agglomerate, thus leading to irregular properties throughout the material.

3.1.4 Composite manufacturing process

Selection of the most suitable composite manufacturing process is dependent on the factors such as the type of reinforcement, the desired properties of the product, size and shape of the end product, manufacturing cost, etc. Therefore, a good balance involving all these issues needs to be set in the design process, in order to reach the desired specifications in the final composite

3.2 Manufacturing of textile reinforced composites

It all starts with nature. Composites are available naturally and many are found around us. Wood is a composite material, which is composed of long cellulose polymeric chains held together by lignin, a much weaker constituent. Owing to the flexible structure, the cellulose fibres give wood its ability to bend without breaking, while the lignin binds these chains and makes the structure stiff. Bone is a made up of collagen, a soft form of protein and apatite, a strong but brittle mineral. In hair and fingernails also collagen is found. On its own collagen would not be of much use in the skeleton but when combines with hydroxyapatite it forms composite, a bone and provides the properties that are needed to support the body.

It has a history of more than 3000 years, human beings started manufacturing and using composites. In ancient Egypt, people used to build walls from the bricks made of mud with straw as reinforcing component [2]. Another important application of composites can be seen around 1200 AD from Mongols. Mongolians invented a bow made up of composites. Using a combination of animal glue, bone and wood, bows were pressed and wrapped with birch bark [3]. Today, composites can be fabricated even more according to an integrated design process resulting in the optimum construction according to parameters such as shape, mass, strength, stiffness, durability, costs, etc. [5].

The properties of a composite are governed by both, properties of reinforced material and the matrix; and the way in which the materials are designed and processed. A technique to be used to fabricate the composite is primarily governed by the type of matrix material, thermoset or thermoplastic, followed by matrix material used, reinforcement form, fibre volume fraction, dimensions of the part to be produced, and complexity of the part shape. Thermosetting resin-based methods use matrix material in liquid resin form while it is a molten polymer in the thermoplastic-based composite. Thermosetting composites can be manufactured using a range of methods such as hand lay-up, resin transfer molding, autoclave molding, compression molding, filament winding, resin infusion, and pultrusion. For thermoplastic matrix-based composites, injection molding and thermoforming are the most commonly used techniques [11]. Various methods of composite fabrication are described below,

3.2.1 Hand Lay-up

It is the simplest and most common manual technique for composite manufacture. The first step in composite production is the application of surface-release agents on the surface of the mound to ensure easy removal of the produced part. After the application of the release agent, a gel coat can be applied to the mound surface for the high-quality part surface. Then, the reinforcement material, in the form of fibres, fabrics, mats, etc., is placed inside the mound, and the resin-hardener mixture is applied on the surface of this reinforcement with the aid of a brush. Then, the entrapped air is removed, and the fabric surface is evened using a roller. Composites are then cured by various methods viz. at room temperature, applying heat, by means of a vacuum, etc. Finally, the cured part is removed from the mound.

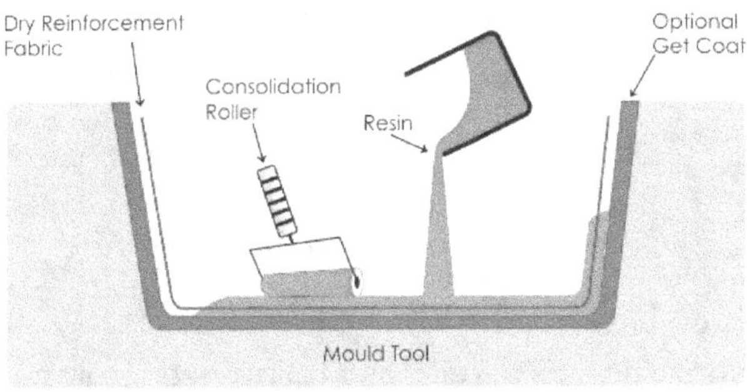

Figure 2.1 Hand lay-up [16]

3.2.2 Resin transfer molding

In this process, preforms are prepared. These preforms are placed in molds and the mound is closed. The resin in the required quantity is then transferred into the mound under pressure. The composite is allowed to cure at suitable conditions. Instead of pumping the resin under pressure, if it is drawn into a preform through the use of a vacuum, the process is called vacuum-assisted resin transfer molding. Unlike resin transfer molding where the resins and catalysts are premixed, reaction injection molding injects a rapid-cure resin and a catalyst into the mound in two separate streams, mixing, and the resulting chemical reaction, occur in the mound.

3.2.3 Autoclave molding

To maximize the performance of a composite part fibre to resin ratio can be increased with followed by removal of air voids. So, thermoset composite materials, produced by hand layup method, are cured in elevated pressures and temperatures at a slow rate. The composite part is kept in a vacuum bag, and vacuum is applied to remove the air bubbles.

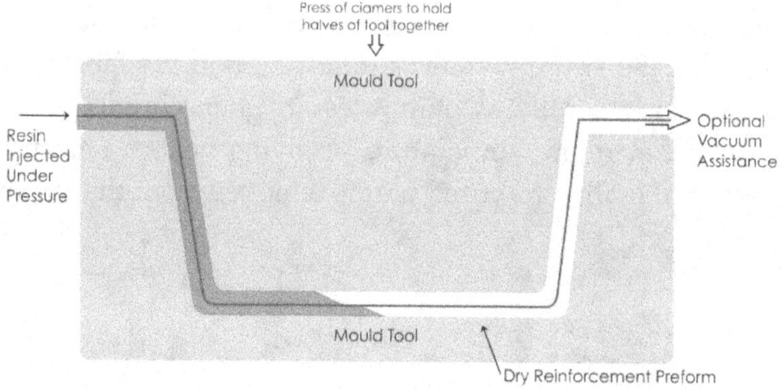

Figure 2.2 Resin transfer moulding [16]

3.2.4 Compression molding

Thermoplastic, as well as thermosets composites, are fabricated by this technique. A compression molding press is used to apply high pressures and temperatures. Pre-impregnated fibres, fabrics, and/or mats, etc. can be used as the starting material and are kept in metallic dies. The curing process typically starts with the application of heat and pressure and generally takes a few minutes. The metallic die is opened after curing and the textile reinforced composite part is removed.

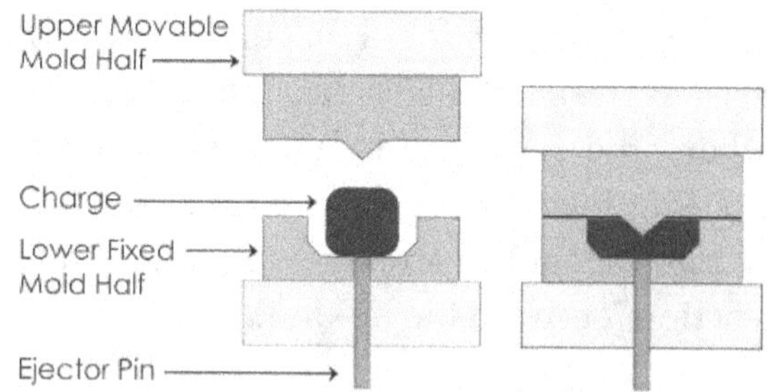

Figure 2.3 Compression molding [17]

3.2.5 Filament Winding

This is a continuous, automated and repeatable process, with relatively low material costs. Continuous filaments are passed through a resin bath before they are wound. This process results in high circumferential strength so is used to produce cylindrical parts such as long composite pipes for liquid transportation, cylindrical rods, etc.

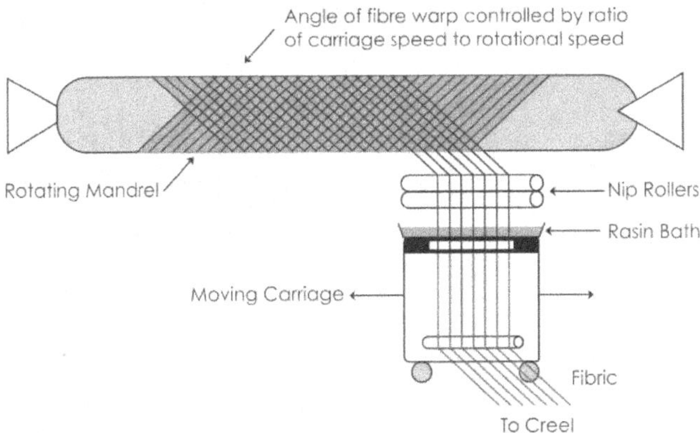

Figure 2.4 Filament winding [16]

3.2.6 Pultrusion

In this very fast and economic composite production process, the reinforcing material is pulled through a heated resin bath, containing a thermoset resin and then moves through a heated die, where it takes its net shape and cures. This composite is then cut to specific length. Fabrics may also be introduced into the die to provide directional reinforcement. Long composite silhouettes of constant cross-section viz. beams used construction, bridges, etc. are produced with this method.

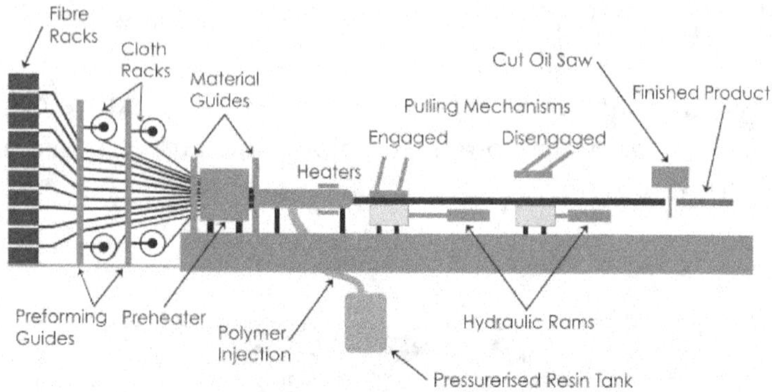

Figure 2.5 Pultrusion [16]

3.2.7 Injection molding

Injection molding is a fast, high-volume, low-pressure, closed process to fabricate composites from a thermoplastic such as polystyrene, nylon, polypropylene etc. [18]. Reinforcement is done by short fibres or particulates. The molding compound in pellet form is composed of short fibres and a thermoplastic matrix. This is then, heated in the injection chamber of the extruder. Heat and shearing action of the screw melts the material. The melted material is then injected into a die under high pressure. After a short cooling cycle, the part is removed from the mound.

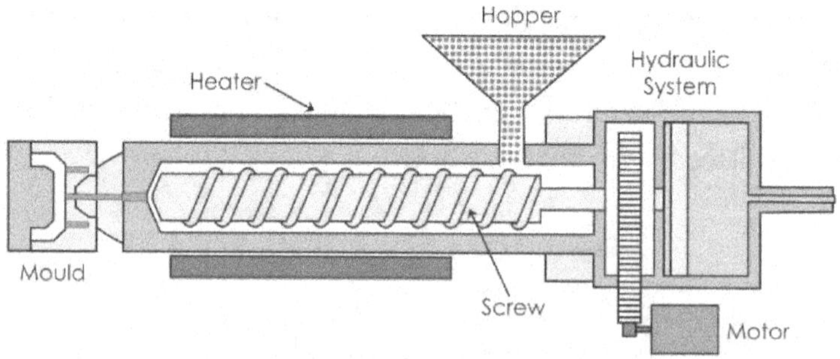

Figure 2.6 Injection moulding [18]

3.2.8 Vacuum infusion

In this process, a large mound made of wood or plastic is generally used. The fabrics are laid up as a dry stack of materials inside the mound cavity and then vacuum bagged, to prevent the entrance of air from the sides. A vacuum pump evacuates the air inside the bag creating atmospheric pressure on the fabric and at the same time resin is allowed to flow into the l into the mound cavity. The vacuum is stopped, when the fabric is sufficiently wetted out by the resin, the part is, then, allowed for curing at room temperature.

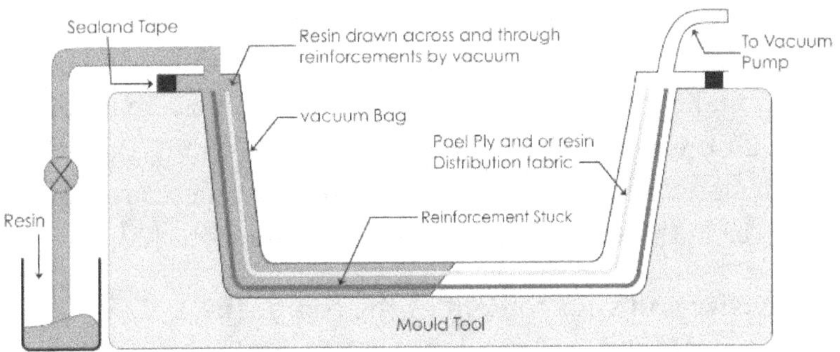

Figure 2.7 Vacuum infusion [16]

3.3 Testing of textile reinforced composites

When first introduced to mechanical testing of composite materials, one can be confused, even overwhelmed, by the number of available test standards. One reason for this large variety of tests is the number of stiffness and strength properties that must be determined. Differences between tests include the size and shape of the test specimen, the manner in which the load is applied to the specimen, and the procedure followed when performing the test. Having identified candidate standardized test methods and developed an understanding of their capabilities, the final selection of the test method most suitable for a particular situation typically is based on a variety of considerations:

a) The composite material to be tested, including the type of constituents (fibre and matrix) and the material form (continuous or discontinuous fibre, unidirectional, random mat, woven, etc.)

b) The material or structural properties desired - stiffness properties, strength properties, or both.

c) The time, equipment and expertise required to perform the test.

Perhaps the most important consideration, however, is the intended use of the test results. When intended for use in quality control or for comparative testing of candidate materials, the simplicity of the test method and its ability to identify material variations are important considerations [19]. Composite tests have been standardized by a number of organizations. The main international composite testing standards are those maintained by ASTM, ISO, etc. In many cases, the test methods described by different standards are basically the same, but there are significant differences in the specimen and fixture dimensions [20].

3.3.1 Density and void content of the composite

Density plays a key role in designing an engineering component or deciding the application of a material, particularly where weight is an important factor. *Actual density,* ρac, Of the composites, is determined by measuring weithe ght and volume of the composite sample. Theoretical density, ρct, is calculated by, using the following formula.

$$\rho ct = \frac{1}{\dfrac{Wf}{\rho f} + \dfrac{Wm}{\rho m}}$$

Where,

- Wf = Fibre weight fraction;
- Wm = Matrix weight fraction
- ρf = Density of fibre;
- ρm = Matrix density

The void content Vv, in a composite, can be estimated by comparing the theoretical density with its actual density.

$$Vv = \frac{\rho ct - \rho ac}{\rho ct}$$

3.3.2 Hardness of composite

Hardness is a measure of material's resistance to permanent deformation or damage, considered as one of the most important factors that govern the wear resistance of materials. There are 6 types of hardness indentation tests used to determine the macro hardness and micro hardness of materials such as metals, ceramics, and plastics. The indenters are much harder than the specimen, and they are smooth balls, cones with hemispherical tips, and pyramidal having three or four faces. The macro hardness indentation testers are the Brinell, Meyer and Rockwell, and the micro hardness indenters are the Berkovich, Knoop and Vickers.

In the Vickers micro hardness test [21], a diamond indenter, in the form of a square-based pyramid with an angle of 136^0 between the opposite faces at the vertex, is pressed into the polished surface of the test specimen. After the force has been removed, the diagonal lengths of the indentation d1 and d2 are measured with an optical microscope. The Vickers microhardness will be denoted as Hardness value (HV).

The Vickers hardness number/Hardness value is calculated by the following formula,

$$VHN = \frac{2F}{d^2} sin\frac{136^0}{2}$$

Where, d is mean diagonal.

$$d = \frac{d_1 + d_2}{2}$$

3.3.3 Tensile Strength

ASTM D638 [22] covers the determination of the tensile properties of unreinforced and reinforced plastics in the form of standard dumbbell-shaped test specimens. It is used to measure the force required to break a polymer composite specimen and the extent to which the specimen stretches or elongates to that breaking point.

3.3.4 Flexural Strength

The flexural test; ASTM D7264 [23], measures the force required to bend a beam under a three-point loading system utilizing center loading on a simply supported beam or a four-point loading system utilizing two load points equally spaced from their adjacent support points, with a distance between load points of one-half of the support span. In this test, the composites cut according to the sample size and were tested to get the results for flexural strength and bending elongation.

3.3.5 Machinability

Machinability is a term indicating how the work material responds to the cutting process. In the most general case, good machinability means that material is cut with the good surface finish, long tool life, low force and power requirements, and low cost [24]. The main goal of machining is to remove material to produce a component or product efficiently. Drilling is one of the oldest and most common machining operations, hole diameters within the range 10 to 20 mm [25].

3.3.6 Moisture Absorption

Moisture Absorption of Matrix Composites is tested by a gravimetric test, ASTM D5229 [26], a method that monitors change over time of moisture content by measuring the total mass change of a coupon that is exposed to a standard testing atmosphere. The specimens are then dried in an oven, and allowed to cool in a desiccator. The specimens are then weighed on an analytical balance to the nearest 0.1 mg. The specimens are then placed in the appropriate conditioning environment allowed to equilibrate and then weighed.

The average amount of absorbed moisture in a material, taken as the ratio of the mass of the moisture in the material to the mass of the oven-dry material and expressed as a percentage Moisture Content (%), calculated using the following formula,

$$Moisture\ Content\ \% = \frac{(Weight\ of\ Moisture)}{Oven\ dry\ weight} \times 100$$

3.3.7 Water Absorption

Water absorption determines the amount of water absorbed under specified conditions with ASTM D570 [27]. For the water absorption test, the specimens are dried in an oven and then placed in a desiccator to cool. Immediately upon cooling the specimens are weighed. The sample is then placed in a container of distilled water maintained, at a temperature of 23 +/- 1°C in water for 24 hours. Specimens are removed, patted dry with a lint-free cloth, and weighed. Water absorption is expressed as an increase in weight percentage.

$$Water\ Absorption\ \% = 100 \times \frac{(Wet\ weight\ -\ Dry\ weight)}{Dry\ weight}$$

3.3.8 Acoustic Test

Acoustical are engineered into room acoustics, industrial noise control, studio acoustics and automotive acoustics and are used as interior lining for apartments, automotive, aircraft, ducts, enclosures for noise equipment and insulations for appliances. Nowadays, more and more one tends to obtain new sound absorbing materials with appropriately good properties of sound absorption. Textiles composite material absorbs sound based on its characteristics, in turn, governed by matrix and reinforcement [28] [29] [30] [31]. Acoustic properties of a material are measured by Impedance Tube Method, wherein, sound waves are confined within the tube. In the case of composites, sound absorption is small for low frequencies and usually increase with increasing frequency.

The noise reduction % is calculated as follows [32]:

$$Noise\ Reduction = \frac{dBwos\ -\ dBws}{dBwos} \times 100$$

Where,

- $dBwos$ = Sound level without sample
- $dBws$ = Sound level with sample

CHAPTER 4
NONWOVEN AS REINFORCEMENT IN COMPOSITE

4.1 Nonwovens overview

"A low-cost alternative for traditional woven or knitted goods" originally the nonwovens were considered as. The objective was to eliminate the whole process of spinning the yarn and then weaving or knitting into the fabric. These fibrous materials were being made ready to use from dry-laid carded webs, binding them using different techniques viz. chemical, mechanical or thermal.

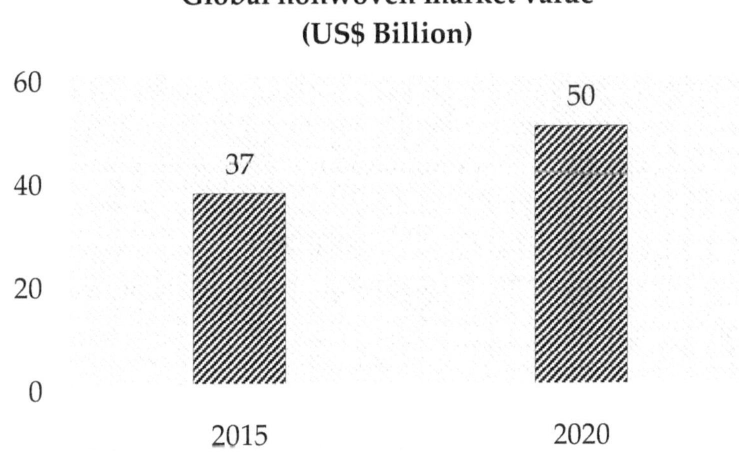

Figure 2.8 Global nonwoven market value (US$ Billion) [33]

As the world is a changing place, so is the development of nonwovens and this growth in nonwoven materials is one of the greatest innovations in the textile industry. Today, various nonwoven technologies enable researchers to ascertain new simple and economical technical solutions. And these innovative nonwoven materials can serve as the basic transferor and structure provider in numerous applications. Thus, nonwovens represent the highest growth segment in the textiles field. Over the last decade, the extent of textile fibre used as a part of nonwoven has surpassed fibre use for woven, knitted and other textile products. The growth in nonwovens is because of growing technological advancements, new product developments and raising awareness among consumers and their pace in adopting nonwoven goods. Growing hygiene and medical industries are also supporting the nonwoven market growth, particularly in the Asia-Pacific and Latin American regions. The Asia-Pacific region is expected to play a major role for the nonwovens market primarily due to emerging economies in China and India, accompanied with growing awareness among customers about the benefits of nonwoven products [33].

The nonwoven technology exists to approximate the appearance, texture, and strength of conventional woven and knitted fabrics due to their simple production stages, high efficiency of production, lower cost, and disposability. Multi-layer nonwoven composites, laminates, and three-dimensional nonwoven fabrics are commercially produced. Nonwovens combined with other materials have different chemical and physical properties. Therefore, nonwovens can be used with a wide variety of industrial engineering, consumer, and health-care goods [34].

4.2 Nonwoven definitions

Nonwovens are defined by ISO standard 9092 and CEN EN 29092. These two documents, identical in their content, are the only internationally acknowledged definition of Nonwovens. EDANA (The European Disposables and Nonwovens Association) has also adopted the definition of nonwoven as per ISO 9092. As industry, trade and technology have evolved since their publication in 1988, these standards are being updated by ISO experts to better reflect what the present understanding of Nonwovens is [35]. As per ISO 9092:2011, [36], nonwoven is a manufactured sheet, web or batt of directionally or randomly orientated fibres, bonded by friction, and/or cohesion and/or adhesion, excluding paper and products which are woven, knitted, tufted, stitch-bonded incorporating binding yarns or filaments, or felted by wet-milling, whether or not additionally needled. The fibres may be of natural or man-made origin.

Nonwovens are broadly defined as sheet or web structures bonded together by entangling fibre or filaments (and by perforating films) mechanically, thermally, or chemically. They are flat, porous sheets that are made directly from separate fibres or from molten plastic or plastic film. They are not made by weaving or knitting and do not require converting the fibres to yarn. Beyond simple definitions, these engineered fabrics open up a world of innovative possibilities for all types of industries. Nonwovens may be a limited-life, single-use fabric or very durable fabric. Nonwoven fabrics provide specific functions such as absorbency, liquid repellency, resilience, stretch, softness, strength, flame retardancy, washability, cushioning, filtering, bacterial barriers and sterility. These properties are often combined to create fabrics suited for specific jobs while achieving a good balance between product use-life and cost. They can mimic the appearance, texture and strength of a woven fabric, and can be as bulky as the thickest paddings [37]. As per American Society for Testing and Materials, [38], the nonwoven is defined as a textile structure produced by bonding or interlocking of fibres, or both, accomplished by mechanical, chemical, thermal, or solvent means, and combinations thereof.

4.3 Fibres for nonwovens

Man-made fibres are the most widely used in the nonwoven industry. Owing to impurities and higher costs, natural fibres are of minor importance for the production of nonwovens. In the field of nonwoven applications, polypropylene and polyester fibres account major share [39].

4.3.1 Polyester fibre

As its name indicates, polyester fibre consists of macromolecules of esters, made of acids and alcohol. If any of these basic molecules are combined, they will form polyesters. While producing nonwoven materials, physical properties of polyester fibres are important. For example, the lengths of cut. Cross section, lustre, etc. They are inexpensive, easily produced from petrochemical sources, and have a desirable range of physical properties. They are strong, lightweight, easily dyeable and wrinkle resistant and have very good wash wear properties. Therefore, polyester fibre is mostly used in nonwoven production. Nonwoven polyester fibre mats are used to produce electrical insulation laminates and electrical tape backing appliances. Polyester and high temperature-resistant m-aramid nonwoven mats are used as a cost-efficient interchange for aramid paper for insulation composites [34].

4.3.2 Polypropylene fibre

Polypropylene has established itself as a very useful industrial and household fibre. However, it has not made a very significant impact in the apparel sector mainly due to its hydrophobicity lock of dyeability and slightly waxy handle. Polypropylene nonwovens are increasingly being used as filter fabrics for wet filtration in the chemical and pharmaceutical industries. Industrial applications also include medical and surgical disposables. Polypropylene spun bonded fabrics are used in a variety of end uses, which include absorbent product cover stock markets, home furnishing and automotive markets because of lowest cost, and in low polypropylene nonwoven fabric applications [34].

4.3.3 Glass fibre nonwovens

Glass fibre is an inorganic non-metallic man-made fibre. Generally, the glass is defined as the frozen state of a super-cooled and thus solidified liquid. In general, textile glass fibres have a high tenacity at a low elongation combined with extremely low density. This results in favourable tenacity or modulus values relative to their weight. Glass fibre is brittle, but in drawing very thin fibres (with a diameter of several microns) from molten glass, a fibrous material is obtained, having a flexibility sufficient for textile processing and utilization as a finished product. Glass fibre mats are excellent heat and noise insulation materials. They are capable of withstanding temperatures above 150°C. Textile glass as a mineral material is naturally inflammable and does not release steam or poisonous gases when subjected to heat. Glass staple fibres are used for the reinforcement of plastics and building materials for insulation and so forth [34].

4.4 Nonwovens manufacturing process

Manufacturing of basic nonwoven structures is mainly two-step process viz. formation of the fibrous web, and then after bonding of the fibrous webs to convert these unstable webs into an integral structure, either mechanically, with the help of chemicals or using thermal energy. Further depending upon the exact needs of consumers, these basic nonwovens undergoes different processes. To impart special features in these basic nonwoven structures, bonding is followed by finishing, which may include calendaring, coating, laminating, embossing, anti-static properties, anti-microbial properties, flame retardant properties, water-repellent properties, etc. The manufacturing steps are described below:

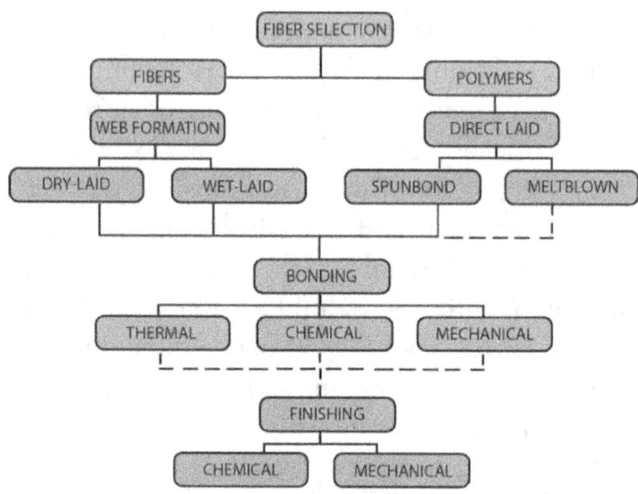

Figure 2.9 Nonwoven manufacturing

Followings are the steps to form nonwoven structures,

1. Web Formation
2. Web Bonding
3. Finishing of the nonwoven sheet

4.4.1 Web Formation

Formation of fibrous web or sheet is a key factor towards physical properties of the end product. These systems are as described below,

A) Web Formation- Fibrous material

Based on fibre length, fibres are converted into web either by laying them in a dry state or in the wet state.

a) Dry laid web

The dry laid web can be produced by two methods viz. carding and air laying.

Carding

In this method, fibres are fed to the machine, wherein those are opened, blended and sent further by air transport for combing with the help of a rotating drum or series of drums, with fine wires points. While lying, if the fibres are laid in the direction of the web travel, the web resultant web is called as parallel-laid and if those are laid randomly, with an orientation not in specific direction, they are known as random-laid.

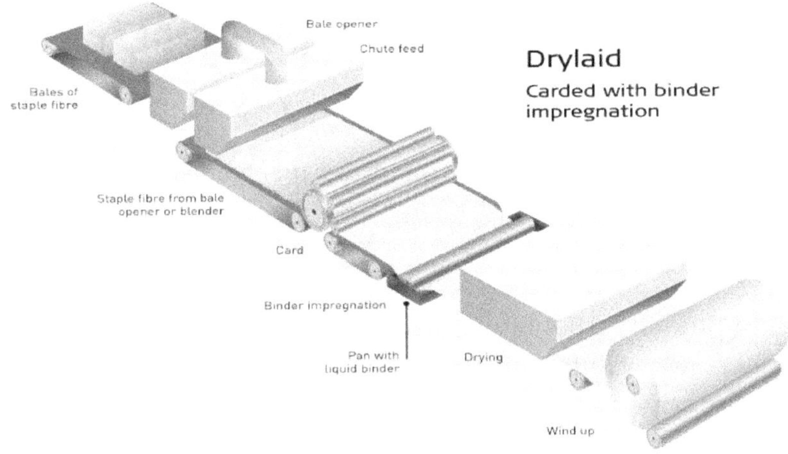

Figure 2.10 Dry laid web preparation [35]

Air laying

In this method, fibres are randomly oriented into the web and are produced by feeding the fibres into an air stream and then to a running belt or perforated drum for compacting the structure. Through this technique, comparatively lighter and softer webs are produced.

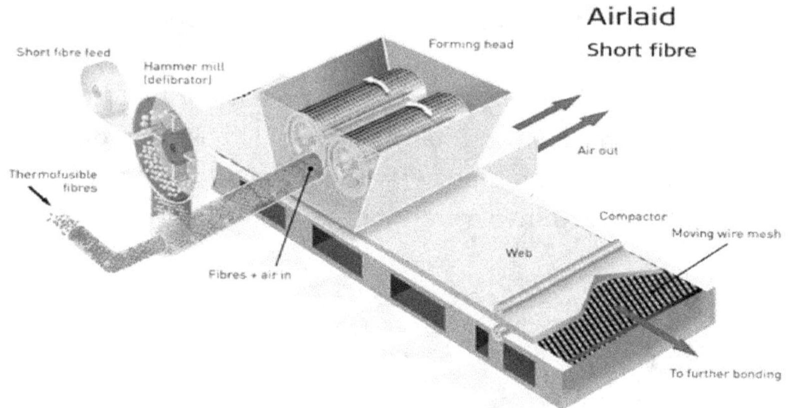

Figure 2.11 Air laid web preparation [35]

Wetlaid web

To produce random oriented, wetlaid webs, fibres are mixed in water and a dilute slurry is prepared. This slurry is then placed on a wire screen which moves continuously, while in, and drains the water to form a web. Then this web is passed through the rollers to remove surplus water, consolidate the web and dry the structure, often followed by impregnation with binders.

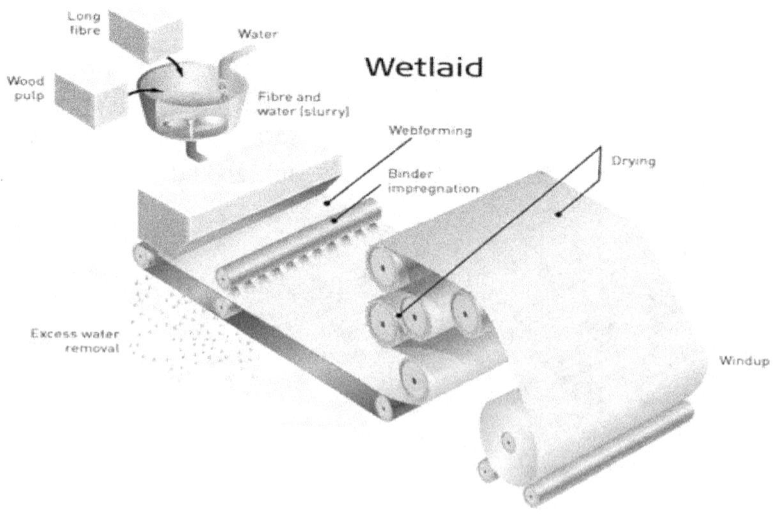

Figure 2.12 Wetlaid web preparation [35]

B) Web formation- Polymeric material

Instead of fibrous raw material, if thermoplastic polymers are used to produce web, then spunmelt technique, is used. It covers spunlaid and meltblown methods.

Spunlaid / Spunbond

In this process, filaments are extruded through spinneret after the polymer is melted at a suitable temperature, followed by cooling and placing them on to a conveyor, to get an even web of continuous filaments.

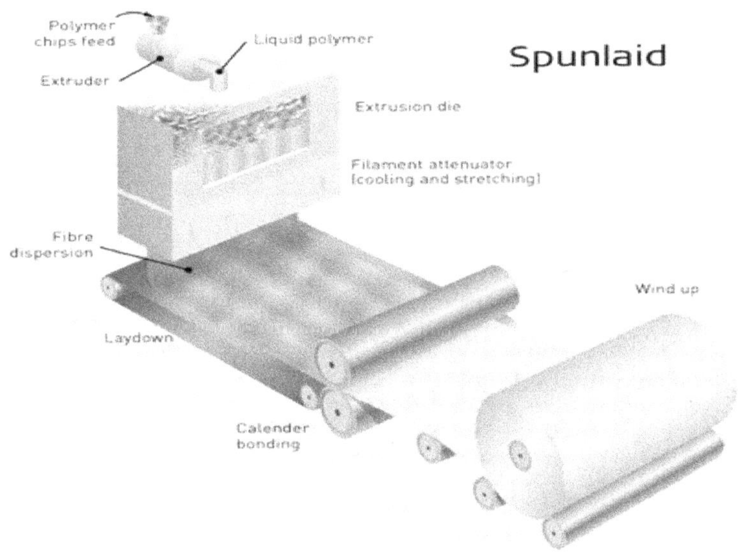

Figure 2.13 Spunlaid web preparation [35]

Meltblown

In this method, low viscosity polymer is extruded through the spinneret. This polymeric solution, immediately after leaving, enters into a high-velocity air-stream and the extruded polymer gets scattered, solidified and results into the web structure.

4.4.2 Bonding of sheet

After the web is formed, it is required to be converted into a consolidated structure. There are three different principles of integrating these webs, viz. Mechanical, chemical and thermal. Nonwoven fabric Properties such as strength, porosity, flexibility, density, etc. are primarily governed by the degree of bonding.

a) Mechanical Bonding

The fibrous web is consolidated mechanically by different bonding technique viz. needle punching, stitch bonding, and hydroentangling. The web structure becomes intact mainly because of the increased inter-fibre friction due to the entanglement of fibres during the act of bonding.

Needle punching

It is a process of forcing the web to mechanically entangle by the reciprocating action of barbed needles through a moving batt of fibres, to produce a nonwoven fabric. The barbed needles are mounted, in a non-aligned fashion, on a board on needles. A nip of rollers or aprons feeds a web of fibrous material continuously, which moves in between the two fixed plates, which are drilled to form holes, to oscillate these barbed felting needles repeatedly through. The punched nonwoven is then consolidated through moving nip roller system. Because of needling action, fibres are entangled gradually to form an intact fabric structure, needle punched nonwoven [39].

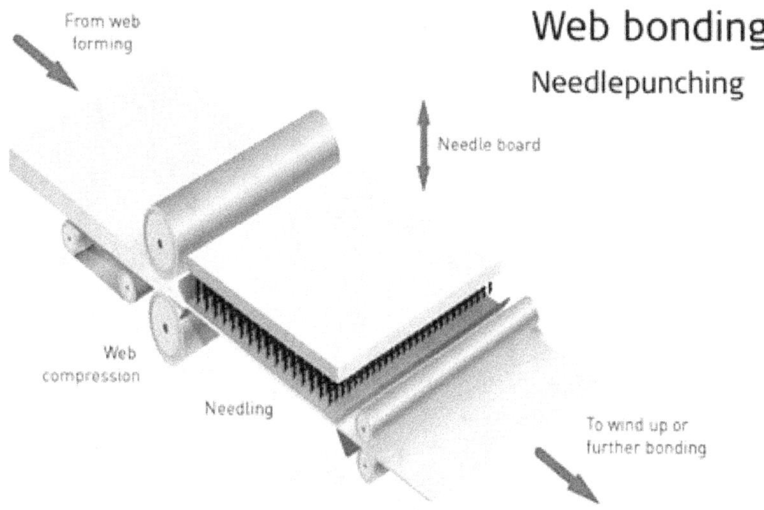

Figure 2.14 Needle punching bonding [35]

Properties of needle-punched nonwoven can be altered by varying properties of incoming material, parameters of web and machine variable. In relation to parameters of the web, weight per unit area, the orientation of fibres in the web and web composition are the factors deciding properties of the needle-punched fabric. The tensile strength of nonwovens is higher in cross direction in comparison with the machine direction, in cross laid nonwovens [40]. The composition of the web includes the type of fibres, properties of fibres like cross-section, surface characteristics, length, fineness, etc. The nature of fibre has a considerable influence on the behavior of nonwovens, during both processing and use. The most important machine variables are the depth of needle penetration and needle punch density; others being the type of needle, barb size and number of passages. The depth of penetration is important because it determines vertical distance through which the needle penetrates the batt on each stroke, thus, fibre entanglement and level of bonding. Thus, punch density and depth of penetration affects the intensity of interlocking and orientation of fibres in punched structure. The punch density defines the number of needle penetrations per unit area and directly affects fabric properties and dimensions. There is a limit beyond which properties of the fabric deteriorate with the increase in these machine variables [41].

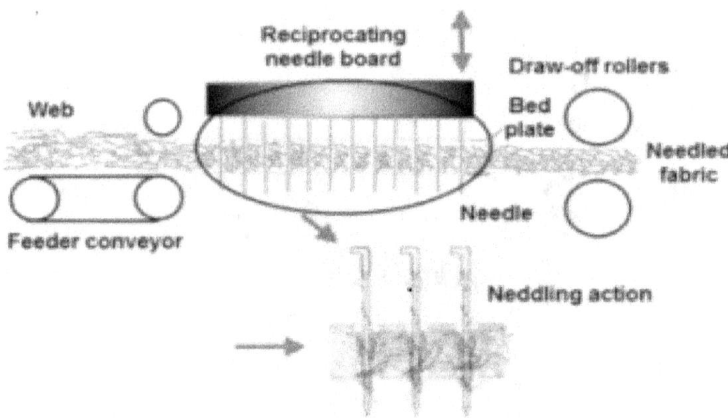

Figure 2.15 Principle of needle punching [42]

b) Hydroentanglement

Hydro-entangling is a method of bonding the web using high-velocity jets of water. The web moves on a conveyor belt at high speed and exposed to the mechanism of entangling because of high-speed water jets. The pressure of water jets is an important factor deciding the extent of entanglement, the orientation of fibres and fibre deformation.

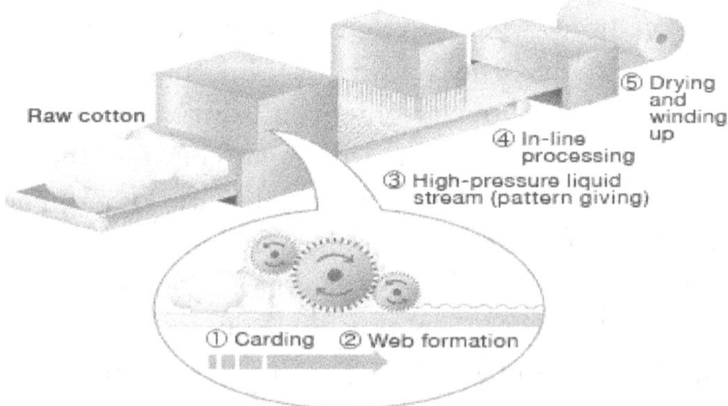

Figure 2.16 Hydroentanglement [35]

The appropriate pressure of water jet is therefore essential to be maintained while bonding, low pressure results into the unstable structure because of inappropriate entanglement of fibres while high pressure results in fibre damage.

c) Thermal Bonding

In this process, the web structure contains thermoplastic fibre, the web passes through heated calendar rollers, and thus thermal energy is used for bonding this web.

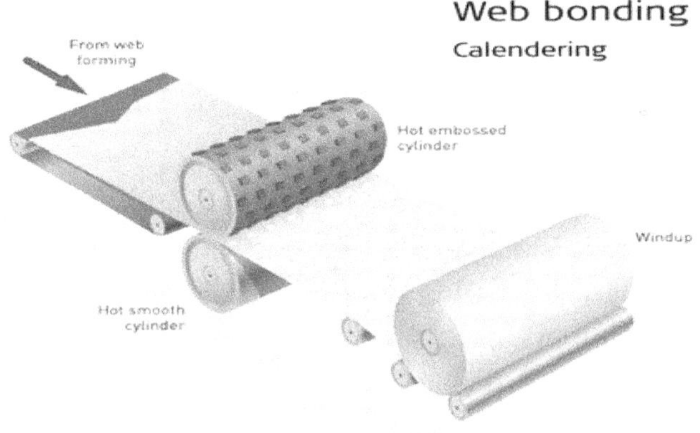

Figure 2.17 Thermal bonding [35]

d) Chemical Bonding

One of the common methods for bonding the web is chemical bonding. Bonding of web structure, in this technique, is done with the help of chemicals. The chemical binder is applied to the fibrous web and then it is cured. Latex, is the most commonly used binder owing to ease of application, the effectiveness of binding and comparatively low cost. Binder is applied on the web by different techniques viz. saturation bonding, spray bonding, print bonding and foam bonding.

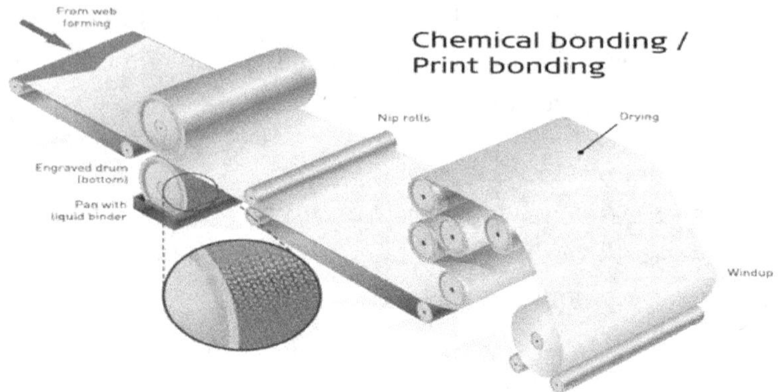

Figure 2.18 Chemical bonding [35]

4.4.3 Finishing and converting of nonwovens

Finishing and converting are the last operations performed on the fabric before it is delivered to the customer. Finishing includes operations such as coating and laminating, calendaring and embossing to impart particular surface properties, corona and plasma treatments to change the wetting properties of the fabric, wet chemical treatments to impart anti-stat" properties, anti-microbial properties, flame retardant properties, etc. After finishing the fabric, it is usually cut to the width the customer specifies a rewound ready for shipment. This is known as converting [35].

4.5 Nonwoven applications [39]

a) Hygiene: Baby diapers and training pants, Adult incontinence pads, Sanitary napkins, Tampons, Nasal strips, Disposable underwear.
b) Wipes: Disposable wipes (dry and pre-moistened), Dusters, Dish clothes, Mops
c) Medical and Surgical: Surgical swabs, wound dressings, surgical gowns, masks and caps, orthopaedic casts, surgical drapes, wraps and packs, Transdermal drug delivery, Heat procedure packs.
d) Protective clothing: Disposable cleanroom garments, Laboratory overalls, Fire protective linings, Thermal

insulation fillings, High visibility clothing, chemical defence suits.

e) Filtration (gas and liquids): Tea Bags, Drinks filtration, Oil sorption, Industrial gas filtration, Respiratory filters, Vacuum filter bags, Odour control.

f) Interlinings and garments: Fusible interlinings and linings, Shoulder pads, Glove linings.

g) Shoe leather goods and coating substrates: Boot and shoe linings, Synthetic leather shoe uppers, Shoe construction components, Luggage and bags.

h) Upholstery furniture and bedding: Ticking, Mattress pads, Waddings and fillings, Sheets and blankets, Window blinds, Quilts backings, Dust covers.

i) Floor coverings: Contract carpets and carpet tiles, Underlays and carpet backing fabrics, automotive carpets and trims.

j) Building and roofing: House wrap, Thermal and sound insulation, Roof linings, under slating, Plasterboard facings, Pipe wraps, Fabric tiles (singles).

k) Civil engineering and geosynthetics: Landfill membrane protectors, Drainage systems, lining systems for reservoirs and pond, Erosion control and ground stabilization, Soil-separation.

4.6 Concept of composite nonwovens

Composite nonwovens are the category of materials to bring the fibres and/or filaments of different types or species or different individualities or a combination thereof, produced by modern and innovative manufacturing techniques using nonwoven technologies or integration of nonwoven and allied technologies. Combinations of different nonwoven, preforms or fabrics, prepared either by employing a variety of different process technologies or by combining nonwoven preforms or fabrics with traditional textile preforms or fabrics or scrims or foams or other materials into a consolidated structure, can also result in the development of composite nonwovens. An embedded phase of particulates, when is incorporated into a matrix phase of fibres or filaments, it forms a three- dimensional network around the particulates and creates composite nonwovens [43]. INDA/EDANA (2005), defines as a nonwoven material; if the essential part cannot be identified, the term composite nonwoven is used when the mass of the nonwoven content is greater than the mass of any other component material. Further, EDANA added that a composite nonwoven may be an unbounded nonwoven preform to which fi laments or spun yarns have been incorporated.

Composite nonwovens as a marriage of two different technologies in one process line or combination of multiple substrates (combination of different types of nonwovens or combination of nonwoven with another type of fabric like a woven or a film) made on entirely different lines.

Nonwoven trade uses the phrase 'composite' for those nonwovens which are either produced by combining laminates of fibres of different types/species (or fibres blended with particulates), or combining laminates of different fibre species with layers of different fibres produced by employing the same technology or different technologies, to obtain a new unified or integrated structure. Composite nonwovens are classified based on raw materials used and process technologies used for manufacturing, as follows,

4.6.1 Multi- fibre/ filament composite nonwoven

This is prepared by mixing the fibres or filaments, different types/species /characteristics/ combination thereof, intimately or in the form of layers of different fibres or filaments to the fibre web, e.g. Nonwoven fabric prepared by combining two webs, one made up of synthetic fibres or filaments and the other made up of natural fibres or filaments.

4.6.2 Particulate composite nonwovens

To prepare particulate composite nonwovens, particulate

matters of interest viz. antimicrobials, antistatic, preservatives, metal particles, fire retardants, waterproofing particles, etc. are embedded into nonwoven structures, e.g. antimicrobial agent like chitosan embedded into meltblown nonwovens.

4.6.3 Hybrid composite nonwovens

When technologically varying materials like woven fabrics, knitted fabrics, braids, films, scrims, foams, etc. are combined with nonwoven fabric, hybrid nonwovens result, e.g. nonwoven for acting as a substrate for artificial leather.

4.6.4 Multi-formed composite nonwovens

More than one forming section like processes include multi-card, multi- forming box air- lay, multi- forming box wet- lay, combinations of various forming processes, etc., adding different fibres/filaments to the web, produces Multi-formed composite nonwovens e.g. a carded web comprised of synthetic fibres and a wet- laid web of short natural fibres and then bonding by employing the hydroentanglement process.

4.6.5 Multi- bonded composite nonwovens

When a set of nonwoven fabric is bonded by a combination of nonwoven bonding processes, it creates multi- bonded composite nonwovens, e.g. nonwoven fabrics bonded by a combination of needle punching and hydroentanglement.

4.6.6 Laminated composite nonwovens

Laminating many nonwoven substrates consisting of either different types of fibres/filaments or nonwovens with other substrates, including woven fabric, knitted fabric, braided fabric, etc. produces a laminated composite, e.g. laminated composite nonwoven comprised of a spunbond layer and a wet- laid layer.

4.6.7 Nonwoven reinforced composites

Nonwoven Reinforced composites are the composite structures, consisting of resinous matrix like epoxy, polyester, etc. reinforced by an embedded nonwoven fabric [44]. Thus, textile structures in the form of nonwoven fabrics, when used as reinforcement in designing of composites, they are called as nonwoven reinforced composites.

Though, direct use of fibres and yarns in making the composite structures might be cheaper in terms of materials costs, handling of these materials is quite difficult. Also, complex component shapes are difficult to be formed with such structures [5]. The woven and knitted structures are more common in textile fabrics. These structures can be seen used in composites. However, woven and knitted structures have few limitations to be used as reinforcements in composites. Because of two dimensional structure, regular woven or knitted structures have limitations in terms of low thickness and weight [45].

Nonwoven fabric, if used as reinforcement offers several advantages over conventional fibre reinforcement i.e. fibre, yarn, two dimensional woven or knitted structures, etc. The nonwoven fabric production process involves lesser process steps compared to conventional weaving, knitting or similar textile formation processes. The nonwoven production process is fundamentally faster in terms of linear output. Nonwovens, [39] can offer relatively low-cost reinforcement, compared to conventional textile preforms. Thus, nonwovens are good alternatives as the production cost is low and the thickness can be varied easily. Nonwoven fabric materials are composed of a random network of overlapping fibres. Nonwovens, unlike reinforcement in the form of fibres, exhibit z-directional properties. Because of the contribution towards z-axis, nonwovens as a reinforcement enhances specific characteristics to composites. An engineer has huge scope to design and develop various types of composites reinforced with nonwovens, to suit specific requirements of the final product. A better understanding of reinforcing the material, type of matrix, manufacturing methodology, etc. enables the production of new textile-based composites for a wide range of applications. Thus, in making composite structures, nonwovens are popularly used for numerous applications, such as automotive parts, construction sector, packing material, etc., since they enjoy a good blend of load-bearing capacity, lightweight, and controllability compared to conventional composite structures [46].

The interface in the composites is one of the most important factors for good performance. Several thin layers of woven structures in composites create several interface layers with the matrix which also creates different modes of failure. It is possible to reduce the modes of failures by reducing the number of interface layers through thicker nonwovens.

Nonwovens are made from both manmade fibres and natural fibres, but the nonwovens from manmade fibres have a higher market share than the natural fibres. The composites made from natural fibre nonwovens are used in automotive industry to absorb sound waves and give acoustic insulation. However, the physical properties of the natural fibre deteriorate over time due to degradation and therefore the applications are limited. The man-made fibres are durable, resistant to microbial attacks and weathering, and therefore attractive in composite applications. Engineered products such as automotive filters, geotextiles, etc. are produced through nonwoven composites. The nonwoven composites are already explored with respective to automotive headliners, auto interior materials, thermal insulation, acoustic insulation and several other technical and structural applications. Further research in this area combining the theoretical models with practical work can effectively replace several composite materials in various applications [45].

Nonwoven reinforced composites, thus, offers a wide area of research where technologist can alter the properties of the composites, by changing the following parameters,

a) Type of Matrix: Cement, Gypsum, Resins like epoxy, polyester, etc.

b) Fibre and properties of fibres used to manufacture nonwoven: Natural/synthetic fibres, high-performance fibres, filament, etc.

c) Properties of nonwoven fabric: GSM, Fibre orientation, etc.

d) The technology used for nonwoven manufacturing: Needle punching, Thermal bond, etc.

e) Machine parameters on nonwoven manufacturing process: Punch density, depth of penetration, etc. in needle punched nonwovens, Air pressure, Percentage of low melt fibres, etc. in thermal bonding

f) Composite manufacturing technique: Hand lay-up, Pultrusion, etc.

g) Finishing treatments, etc.: Addition of additives like UV resistant, flame retardant, etc.

Since all these parameters affect the properties of the nonwoven reinforced composite, an engineer has a huge scope to design and develop various types of composites reinforced with nonwovens, to suit specific requirements of the final product. A number of products can be developed by varying these parameters. No doubt, polymer-matrix composites are being reinforced extensively by two- and three-dimensional textile assemblies and also being utilized in numerous applications, the study of synthetic nonwoven reinforcements of different structural and compositional formats has been limited [47].

4.8 Needle punched nonwovens for composites

Needle punching, the most common web bonding method, is the method of consolidation of fibrous webs to form a nonwoven structure, by repeated penetration of an array of barbed needles. These needles, owing to the specific shape, carry tufts of the fibres from the fibrous web into a vertical direction through the web. Because of this action, fibres are interlocked in the third or 'Z' dimension and results into an integrated three-dimensional intermingled structure. Needle punched nonwoven finds a huge range of applications such as road and railway construction, landfills, automotive parts, filtration, packing material, carpets, insulation, etc.

In the production of polymer composites, the use of needle punched nonwoven fabric mats is beneficial as these materials improve the toughness and strength of light-weight [48]. To impart mechanical properties in three dimensions, the nonwovens should have out-of-plane deflections of fibres. This out-of-plane deflection can be achieved in mechanically bonded nonwovens [49]. Needle punched nonwoven fabric mat has three-dimensional orientations of fibres due to the interlocking of fibres. The absence of chemical binders or fibre fusion within the fabric structure provides for high porosity as well as a large accessible fibre surface area for matrix-fibre adhesion. They can create multiply connected pores through which the resin can flow easily and interlinked mechanism with fibres taking place [50].

The most common use of needle punching in composite materials is for brittle matrix reinforcement, although thin layers of needle punched web may be useful as inter-plies in a layered fabric composite, or sacrificial surface layers. Needle punched nonwoven materials have an inherent low modulus, so complex shapes also can be formed with these materials Composite applications for such materials include low-cost marine hulls, static reduction plates for laptop computers, and stadium seating [10].

NOTES

CHAPTER 5
INVESTIGATIONS IN NONWOVEN COMPOSITES

Current and future prospective applications for three-dimensional fibre reinforced polymer composites are prepared by the various textile processes viz. weaving, braiding, stitching and knitting. Compared to conventional two-dimensional composites, 3D textile composites have a vast range of properties that are superior to former. Conversely, to date, these properties have not been exploited for many applications. Structures that have been made to demonstrate the possible uses of 3D composites include applications in aircraft, marine craft, automobiles, civil infrastructure and medical prosthesis [47].

Polypropylene offers a number of favourable characteristics for high volume applications because of its low price, high toughness and low density. Moreover, polypropylene can easily be processed, recycled, and upgraded via the use of glass fillers which has successfully bridged the gap between the commodity polypropylene composites and the engineering thermoplastics. Nonwoven fleeces of polypropylene fibre and hemp fibres of different blending ratios were prepared in the study conducted by Hajnalka Hargitai et al., [51]. After carding the thin layers were bonded by a needle punching machine. Composite sheets were then prepared by hot pressing of hybrid mats at a temperature of 190ºC. The effect of fibre content and the anisotropy in nonwoven mat resulting from the carding technology were examined. It is observed that fibre proportion in blend does affect mechanical properties of the composite.

To compare the reinforcement capacities of a modified polypropylene when it is reinforced by layers of flax fibres, Martin Nicolas et al. [52], examined three different technologies, which allow reinforcements to be produced with fibres randomly oriented in the laminate plane: these are non-woven produced by spun lacing or needle punching, and mats produced by paper processing techniques. Composite plates were manufactured by compression moulding. The film stacking method was used. Sheets of non-woven and matrix films were stacked and then moulded. The study reveals that the structure of non-woven reinforcements is strongly dependent on the manufacturing route. By varying the fibre content it was observed that the most efficient reinforcement for flax fibres is the mat produced by paper processing.

A composite with flax nonwoven fabrics with different thicknesses was prepared and their cement infiltration was evaluated by Josep Claramunt et al. [53]. Flax-cotton fibres were used to prepare the nonwoven structures, using the double needle-punching machine. These nonwovens than are used as reinforcement in cement matrix to prepare composites by pressing method. It was reported that use of nonwoven flax fabrics as reinforcement in cement-based composites leads to cement materials with very high ductility. Nonwoven structures with low thickness and high entanglement, in the form of multilayer reinforcement, allow a higher infiltration of the cement paste through the nonwoven promoting higher fibre-matrix adherence.

A.H.M Fazle Elahi et al. prepared glass fibre reinforced unsaturated polyester-based polymer composite using hand layup process [54]. The main objective of this experiment is to investigate the influence of various temperature levels of glass fibre reinforced unsaturated polyester composite. Four plies of glass fibre were reinforced to polyester resin and its response to different mechanical properties of the fabricated composite by temperature variations was determined. The composites were found to be temperature sensitive, attributed to the internal change of fibre matrix adhesion of the composite and evolution of the linkage of the resin due to heat.

Cement matrixes are brittle in nature. For this reason, asbestos fibres were applied for cement reinforcement during the last century. Despite all proper properties gained by this reinforcement, it can also constitute a major health hazard to human's safety. H. Pakravan et al., [55], addressed the application of polypropylene nonwoven layers for strengthening cement composite by investigating its flexural performance. Nonwoven layers produced by two different bonding techniques (needle-punching and calendaring) were used to reinforce cement sheets. The polypropylene nonwoven fabrics with different weights at different textile layers were used in cement composites and flexural properties were investigated. The effects of re-punching of needles on nonwoven fabrics performance in the cementitious matrix were also studied. It was shown that both types of nonwoven fabrics show better performance in toughness and load-bearing capacity in comparison to the short fibre. Also, needle-punched specimens displayed better performance in comparison to the calendared specimen since the needle-punched nonwovens have inherently greater open structures with respect to thermo-bonded layers. Repeated punching open the structure of these needle-punched nonwoven fabrics, so punching usage increases the load-bearing capacity of composites. It is concluded that since the volume fraction of fibres was a sensitive and important parameter that affects composites performance, using nonwoven fabrics can increase fibres' volume content in composites without side effects.

To study the effect of fibre type, fibre linear density and needle punching density on the mechanical properties of the nonwoven reinforced elastomeric composites, Muhammad Tausif et al., [56], compared mechanical properties of nonwoven preform reinforced flexible thermoplastic polyurethane composites with those reinforced with polyphenylene terephthalamide (aramid). It was concluded that reinforcement of thermoplastic polyurethane moulded composites with polyester and lyocell nonwovens led to a minimum 2.5 fold increase in tensile strength compared to unreinforced thermoplastic polyurethane. High strength fibres do not essentially produce high strength nonwoven preforms, with all other parameters constant. The tensile properties of nonwoven-reinforced composites are mainly dependent upon fibre tensile properties and fibre segment orientation distribution. Though the tensile strength of the nonwoven preform does not markedly contribute to the tensile strength of the composite, the structural and dimensional modifications associated with increased levels of bonding such as greater fibre entanglement, fibre re-orientation, fabric density and fibre volume fractions can influence resulting mechanical properties.

Textile concrete with nonwoven polypropylene fabric can be used for protective layers of reinforced concrete structures, reducing the thickness of the cover layer or reducing the water penetration rate into the structure. J Žák et al. [57], have presented a method of production and application of textile reinforced concrete with polypropylene nonwoven fabric. The material is produced by layering the reinforcing and filler layers. The material is suitable as a protective layer for reinforced concrete structures as many microcracks are created within the protective layer. These structures find application in reducing the cover layer thickness for outdoor structures, rehabilitation of surface layers of structures or reduction of the rate of water penetration into waterproof reinforced concrete structures.

In a study of Coir fibre and nonwoven cement reinforced composite [58], Pooja Katkar et al. studied those composites for their properties viz. Thermal conductivity, Bending strength, Compressive strength and Moisture regain. It was concluded that coir nonwoven made from fibres after boiled is most effective as reinforcement in cement composite, in terms of bending and compressive strength.

In the study conducted by M. Awaad et al. [59], a nonwoven cellulose fabric is used. Viscose rayon nonwoven fabric was treated with chemically pure Aluminium nitrate nonahydrate.

Then the specimens were fired at 600ºC under a flowing air stream. The author concluded that nonwoven cellulose fabric can be successfully used as a template for generating ceramic materials which show many favourable attributes and might be used as high-temperature resistant exhaust-gas cleaning devices, advanced micro-reactor systems and immobilization supports for medical and biotechnological processes.

When nonwovens are reinforced in a suitable matrix, they result in non-woven composites. Xiaoqun Zhang [60], developed a new method of preparing biodegradable all-cellulosic composite nonwoven materials composed of cotton and kenaf or cotton and bagasse. Carding and Needle-Punching were used to form the staple fibre web. The nonwoven composites bonded with cellulose solutions were formed using the "solution coating" method, viz., assembling of fibre web layers and lyocell solution in a "bread and butter" sandwich style, where the web was the "bread" and the cellulose solution (lyocell adhesive) was the "butter", followed by pressing the fibrous webs and the adhesive "sandwich" into a flexible sheet. It has been shown that synthetic polymers can be substituted for the stabilization of nonwovens by a solution of cellulose.

Intimate blending of the binder fibre with cellulosic fibres is the key to the manufacture of composites with good properties. With a focus on producing compostable cotton fibre based composites, M.G.Kamath et al. developed cotton fibre nonwovens for automotive composites [61]. Studies have shown that these natural fibres such as cotton, kenaf, and flax have the ability to form a good bond between thermoplastic binder polymers. Bonding between cotton or natural fibres and the binder polymer is very good when composites are made from mixed fibre or carded webs. The blending of kenaf or flax enhances tensile strength and modulus of the cotton composite. Also for kenaf and flax fibres, adding cotton helps in increasing the tensile elongation of the composites. In addition, it has been concluded that in order to produce biodegradable composites out of natural fibres, both PLA and BioPET are suitable candidates that act as good binders. Techniques such as Air-laying or Carding produce more uniform webs that improve the tensile properties of the composites. As a result, by suitably combining cotton, kenaf, and flax with an appropriate biodegradable binder fibre in the right combination a moldable fabric that is suitable for automotive applications can be produced.

Properties of nonwoven based composite depend among others on technological parameters, mass content and characteristic of filling fibres i.e. polymer, length, linear density, tensile strength, preparation, a kind of matrix material and the level of components' mixing. Nonwovens are the fibrous materials with relatively good acoustic properties because of the great surface area, in comparison with the traditional foams. Eulalia Gliścińska et al. [62], investigate the effect of mass content of filling submicrofibres on the sound absorption property of thermoplastic composites manufactured on the basis of polypropylene or polylactide nonwoven. The filling submicrofibres were obtained in the enzymatic treatment of waste flax fibres. The thermoplastic model composites were obtained from the textile multilayer structure on a hydraulic press machine with a water-cooling system. Results showed that for the same conditions of the composite manufacturing process and similar composite thickness, a gradual increase in the content of filling cellulose submicrofibres leads to adequately increase in the sound absorption coefficient of the composites.

The use of reclaimed fibres has the advantages of consuming less water and chemical products, does not contaminate the subsoil, water or air, consumes less energy, recycle textile garments or fabrics which would otherwise become waste. More eco- friendly composite materials for automotive manufacturing have been made by Mr. S. Sakthivel et al. [63], using reclaimed fibres and recycled polyester fibres, by a compression moulding method. Nonwoven fabric composites made have been found to provide good physical and mechanical properties when compared with the widely used cotton: polyester nonwoven fabric composites, at very competitive price points. These eco-friendly composites that can be compression moulded into a wide range of parts have a greater bending stiffness, is more resistant to fire, less expensive and without the odour problems that accompany many natural fibres.

Nazire Deniz Yilmaz et al. [64], studied the effects of the material and treatment parameters on airflow resistivity and normal-incidence sound absorption coefficient of alkalized three-layered nonwoven composites. Fibre size and porosity, treatment temperature, duration and concentration are the variable factors. Webs of fibres were formed. Three layers of webs were stacked to form Polypropylene/Hemp/ Polypropylene (PHP) nonwoven Structures. Needle-punched fabrics were subjected to alkalization treatment. Alkalization treatment has been found to result in a loss of basis weight and a decrease in airflow resistivity. Among treatment factors, the only temperature was found to be a statistically-significant factor on air flow resistivity. Higher-temperature alkalization leads to higher air flow resistivity compared to the lower-temperature treatment. Alkalization at a higher temperature and higher concentrations gives better results in normalized sound absorption performance compared to lower-temperature and lower-concentration treatments, respectively.

Unlike metals, the mechanical properties of fibre reinforced polymer composites have been observed to be very sensitive to the presence of common organic solvent molecules, which can easily diffuse into the polymer matrix altering the strength of the composites. M.N. Satheesh Kumar et al. [65], studied Castor oil based polyurethane-polyester nonwoven fabric composites by impregnating the polyester nonwoven fabric in a composition containing castor oil and diisocyanate. Composites were fabricated with two different isocyanates such as toluene-2, 4-

diisocyanate and hexamethylene diisocyanate. The diffusion coefficient values of n-alkane penetrants into reinforced polyurethane-polyester nonwoven fabric composites are higher compared to un-reinforced polyurethane. The diffusion and permeation coefficients obtained were found to decrease with increase in the molar volume of the penetrants. The increase in temperature has increased interaction of alkane penetrants with the polyurethane and their composites. The specimens having a lower pore size and void content showed higher activation energy.

Viscose fibre based needle punched nonwoven fabric-reinforced laminated composites were fabricated by Amar Patnaik and Sachin Tejyan [50], using hand lay-up technique with varying mass per unit area of fabric mat and varying fabric mat weight percentage. The effect of varying mass per unit area of fabric mat and the weight percentage of these different fabric mats were reported on mechanical, physical and visco-elastic properties of needle-punched nonwoven reinforced epoxy composites. The comparative analysis shows that both GSM and fabric weight percentage do affect properties of composites significantly. These mechanical and physical properties are also improving with raise in mass per unit area of fabric.

The spun fibres, which may be drawn, are laid down directly onto a belt by needle punching, air laying or carding. Among the various methods of making nonwovens, the needle punching process has the advantage of producing low-density nonwoven mats with good tensile strength, which is essential in making lightweight polymer composites and helps to incorporate a greater amount of polymer matrix into the composite during manufacture. M.N. Satheesh Kumar and Siddaramaiah [66], have reported on composites constructed by impregnating the needle-punched polyester nonwoven fabric in poly (styrene-co-butyl acrylate) latex containing different weight ratios of corn-starch. The thermoplastic composites thus manufactured have been studied for their physicomechanical properties and swelling behaviour in water. The composites manufactured were moulded, and the effects of the starch content on the performance of the moulded composites studied by measuring the percentage area shape retention, hardness, resilience and water resistance. The study concludes that corn starch content can be added up to 20 weight % to manufacture the poly (styrene-co-butyl acrylate)-polyester nonwoven composites.

Anita Grozdanov et al. [67], developed natural fibre non-woven reinforced PLA based eco-composites by a compression moulding method. Flax and kenaf fibres have been used as reinforcement. Flax and kenaf nonwoven preforms have been treated by different surface treatments: dewaxing, vinyl monomer grafting, alkali treatment, and acetylation. The composites are compared for decomposition temperatures and Flexural strength and modulus. Flax based eco composites show higher thermal stability as well as higher flexural strength.

Polypropylene materials, because of their electric properties, mechanical properties and resistance to noxious agents are used in various industries. Polypropylene materials characterise, also, with the lowest specific density among widely used polymers. Those properties predispose polypropylene to be used as a substrate for composite protective screens shielding people and electric or electronic devices against the noxious activity of electromagnetic fields. Maciej Jaroszewski et al. [68], have made the shields for suppression of electric field in the form of composites of polypropylene nonwoven fabrics with deposited plasma layers. Composite shields are fabricated through metallizing film surfaces or polypropylene nonwoven fabric. Due to their lightness and mechanical strength, those composites are an alternative to classic electromagnetic field shielding materials. It was observed that polypropylene in form of nonwoven fabric is a promising material for electromagnetic shield composites. Dielectric response of the composite non-woven polypropylene/plasma layer is a function of both the physical structure of the substrate and applied layer.

Natural plant fibres as reinforcements in polymeric composites provide technological, economic, ecological and environmental benefits over glass fibres reinforcement. The effect of reinforcement on impact properties on hemp reinforced unsaturated polyester composite specimens, varying fibre volume fractions, was studied by H.N. Dhakal et al. [69]. Needle punched randomly oriented nonwoven hemp fibre was used as the reinforcement to prepare the composite samples by hand lay-up method. The result was compared with chopped strand mat E-glass fibre reinforced unsaturated polyester composites. The study concludes that, with an increase in fibre volume fraction, impact resistance of composite increases because of an increased damage propagation phase. It was found that these hemp nonwoven reinforced composites are comparable to equivalent fibre volume fraction of chopped strand mat E-glass fibre reinforced unsaturated polyester composite specimens, in terms of impact resistance.

A significant advance in the performance levels of high-temperature superconducting materials has made them suitable for commercially viable applications such as coils and cables. In recent years, epoxy-based composites reinforced with nonwoven polyester fabric have been developed for high-temperature superconducting applications because of their excellent electrical properties. Nonwoven fabrics provide low-cost reinforcement for composites as alternatives to unidirectional tapes, woven fabrics and braided fabrics, and they have growing applications in composite structures. To characterize the mechanical response of nonwoven polyester/epoxy composites at cryogenic temperatures is the objective of the work carried out by Yasuhide Shindo et al. [70]. The composite specimens were produced from the cylindrical components, and their elastic and strength properties at room temperature and liquid nitrogen temperature were experimentally determined from tension, compression and flexure tests. After testing, failed specimens were observed by microscopy to assess the failure characteristics of the composites. The temperature dependence and anisotropy of the composite properties were examined. The results of this study are helpful in the design of the components of high-temperature superconducting devices.

Henri Kröling et al. [71], compared paper reinforcements with a commercially available flax fibre spun lace reinforcement and a viscose spun lace reinforcement. Both paper and natural fibre spun laces reinforce the resin significantly. It was shown that paper can outperform both spun laces in terms of tensile strength and Young's modulus. Even paper composites made from untreated eucalyptus pulp achieve higher tensile strengths than the spun laces. Furthermore, the tensile strength of paper composites can be strongly increased by refining and fibre orientation. The fibre orientation of the paper leads to a corresponding anisotropy in the composite properties.

In the study conducted by Mehmet Dasdemir et al. [72], commercial fibre grades of polyethylene terephthalate, polyamide-6, and polypropylene were used as the core (reinforcement) polymer. Linear low-density polyethylene and polypropylene were used as the sheath (matrix) polymer. They introduced a new technique to produce engineering thermoplastic composites from bicomponent nonwovens without using any additional resin or binder. The inherent composite structure of the bicomponent fibres, bicomponent nonwoven fibres and nonwovens were produced using the bicomponent spunbonding process. A hot press was used to produce a nonwoven composite. Mechanical performance of nonwoven composites was compared with a composite which has a polypropylene matrix and 40% glass fibre content. Nonwoven composites showed higher specific stress, superior strain at break and impact strength than glass mat reinforced polypropylene thermoplastic composite. From an industrial point of view, this technique permits the transformation of an inexpensive preform into an engineered thermoplastic composite in one step with excellent wetting characteristics of the matrix polymer.

In the study conducted by S. Rassmann et al., non-woven kenaf fibre mats were reinforced in polyester resin by RTM process [73]. It was found that neither drying of fibres nor altering the mould temperature has any significant effect on mechanical properties of non-woven kenaf fibre reinforced polyester laminates. To study the effect of resin on composite properties, S. Rassmann et al. reinforced non-woven kenaf fibre with different GSM in epoxy, polyester and vinyl ester resins by RTM process. It is concluded that mechanical properties of composites such as tensile strength, flexural strength are affected by the type of resin as well as the fibre volume fraction [74]. Polyester laminates showed good modulus and impact properties, epoxy laminates displayed good strength values and vinyl ester laminates exhibited good water absorption characteristics. Polyester laminates have the highest impact energy and strength, followed by the vinyl ester and then the epoxy laminates.

Low-cost nonwoven fabrics can provide effective reinforcement for flat composite panels or parts with a single curvature. The consolidation behaviour of E-glass nonwoven preforms and the mechanical properties of the resulting composites are studied by, Youjiang Wang [75]. The reinforcement structures include stitch-bonded chopped-strand mat, powder-bonded chopped-strand mat, and continuous-strand mat. A woven fabric is also included for comparison. The bulkiness of the fabric influences their processibility in the hand lay-up and resin transfer moulding processes. Mechanical properties of specimens from the hand lay-up and the resin transfer moulding processes are evaluated in tensile, compressive, and flexural tests. Nonwoven composite specimens from manual lay-up and resin transfer moulding seem to show similar failure modes. When adjusted for the differences in fibre volume fraction, they also show similar mechanical properties. The properties of woven fabric reinforced composites, on the other hand, exhibit significant dependence on the consolidation method.

Thermoset composites made from jute woven fabric, jute non-woven mat and jute carded-sliver have been manufactured in the project conducted by Rejaul Hasan and Rishad Rayyaan [76]. For manufacturing different composite laminates, four & nine layers of woven fabric, one & two layers of non-woven mat and three layers of carded sliver have been used. Each of the three different composites exhibited a reinforcing effect to the epoxy matrix system. It has been found that in terms of stiffness sliver reinforced composite shows the highest stiffness and non-woven composites show the lowest stiffness. In terms of strength, non-woven reinforced composite shows the lowest values. The strength of woven and sliver reinforced composites have been found to be almost similar.

The kenaf/polypropylene nonwoven composites with 50/50 blend ratio by weight, were produced by carding and needle-punching techniques, followed by a compression moulding [77]. The influence of manufacturing conditions was investigated by evaluating the mechanical, thermal, and acoustical performance. It was observed that the manufacturing conditions did not significantly affect the composite thermo-mechanical properties. The kenaf/polypropylene nonwoven composites were more thermally stable than virgin polypropylene plastics by adding kenaf fibre as reinforcement.

Nonwoven fabric mat absorbs resin easily because of the high void volume of the fabric and this leads to composites with a uniform distribution of fibres and resin throughout, resulting in excellent mechanical properties. Needle-punched nonwoven fabric mat reinforced composites also offer good inter-laminar, shear and compressive properties. Epoxy resin and polypropylene based needle-punched nonwoven as a reinforced component of composites were fabricated by Sachin Tejyan and Vedant Singh for assessing for solid particle erosion wear behaviour [78]. It was observed that the polypropylene-based needle-punched nonwoven fibre mat reinforced polymer composites have semi ductile erosive wear behaviour during solid particle erosion. Parameters such as sand particle size, impact velocity, impingement angle, material properties like the type of fibre and fibre content, types of the matrix have a strong effect on the erosion wear behaviour of composites.

Noise pollution has become an increasing amount of attention nowadays to scientist, technologist as well to the general public as a whole [79]. A decibel meter is used for measuring of source decibel and the receipt decibel, without and with fabric sample. The sound reduction responsible for fabric which is expressed as the measure of sound insulation, the difference between decibel reduction with material and without material. It was found that polypropylene blended nonwovens reduce noise level significantly. The increase in electromechanical systems in the automotive industry with the development of new technologies has resulted in an increase in noise pollution. Noise pollution poses a significant threat to human comfort. Nonwoven fabrics are ideal materials for use as acoustical insulation products because they have a high total surface. Recently, recycled nonwovens, as one of the most common textile products, have become important sound absorption materials because the waste generated from the nonwoven industry has increased gradually every year and caused many serious problems. Factories that manufacture nonwovens normally dispose of the selvedges by burying and burning, often leading to environmental pollution and destruction. Recycling and reusing fibrous waste is one of the most important environmental tasks that face the world, to reduce environmental loading and promote the most effective use of resources. With the increase in weight per unit area of nonwovens, sound insulation increases, in relation to the decrease in air permeability [80].

Sound absorbing materials used to provide optimal conditions in rooms can be applied in the form of textiles with a special structure such as nonwovens or fibre-containing composites [31]. Nonwovens owing to their great surface are often mentioned beside spacer knitted fabrics as fibrous materials with a relatively good acoustic behaviour, with respect to conventional materials such as foams. However, such materials are not a sufficiently good solution under all application conditions. Sometimes a sound absorbent in the form of a composite meeting specified requirements resulting from exploitation conditions is required to be used. Composites, depending on their structure, can fulfil various expectations connected with their strength, rigidity, resistance, weight, thickness or surface quality. Currently, researchers are focusing on obtaining new sound absorbing materials with appropriately good properties of sound absorption, high stability and resistance to various factors, and with proper form and surface quality. A promising solution, in respect of both economy and acoustic properties of the material obtained, would be the use of waste fibres.

NOTES

CHAPTER 6
BIBLIOGRAPHY

1. D. Das, B. Pourdeyhimi, "Composite Nonwoven Materials: Structure, Properties and Applications", Woodhead publication, Cambridge, UK, 2014.

2. V. K. Thakur, "Green Composites from Natural Resources", CRC Press, Florida, 2014.

3. S. Thomas, C.H. Chan, L. A. Pothen, J. Joy, H. Maria, "Natural Rubber Materials: Volume 2: Composites and Nanocomposites", RSC Polymer Chemistry Series No. 8, The Royal Society of Chemistry, 2014.

4. H. Pal, N. Jit, A. K. Tyagi, S. Sidhu, "Metal Casting- A General Review", Advances in Applied Science Research, 2, 360-371, 2011.

5. K. Van Rijswijk, M.Sc. W.D. Brouwer, M.Sc. Prof. A. Beukers, "Application of Natural Fibre Composites in the Development of Rural Societies", Delft University of Technology, 2001.

6. D. Gay, S. V. Hoa, S. W. Tsai, "Composite Materials: Design and Applications", CRC Press, Florida, 2002.

7. Ihueze, Chukwutoo, C, Obuka, Nnaemeka S.P, "Engineered Composite Materials and Natural Fibres: Design and Manufacture (A Review)", IOSR Journal of Mechanical and Civil Engineering, 13, May- Jun 2016.

8. Emma Bennette Huntley, "Composite Resin Developments: Epoxy resin vs Vinyl ester vs Polyester Use and application overview", www.compresdev.co.uk, 2014.

9. K. Shiva Shankar, Ch Harish, B. Praharshini, Amulya, Rahul, "Fabrication of Fiber Reinforced Composite", International Journal of Innovative Research in Science, Engineering and Technology, 5, July 2016.

10. Pastore, Christopher M, "Opportunities and Challenges for Textile Reinforced Composites", Mechanics of Composite Materials, April 2012.

11. Nesrin Sahbaz Karaduman, Yekta Karaduman, Huseyin Ozdemir and Gokce Ozdemir, "Textile Reinforced Structural Composites for Advanced Applications", 10.5772/intechopen.68245

12. "Overview of Fiber-Reinforced Composites", http://web.mit.edu/course/3/3.064/www/slides/composites_overview.pdf.

13. A. C. Long, "Design and manufacture of textile composites", Woodhead Publishing, Cambridge, UK, 2005.

14. K. L. Pickering, M. G Aruan Efendy, T. M. Le, "A review of recent developments in natural fibre composites and their mechanical performance", Composites Part A: Applied Science and Manufacturing, 83, 98–112, April 2016.

15. R. Velmurugan, "Composite Materials, Micro-mechanics of Lamina", Dept. of Aerospace Engg., Indian Institute of Technology, Madras, nptel.ac.in.

16. https://netcomposites.com/guide-tools/guide/manufacturing

17. http://www.ino-via.com/index.php/cn/blog/145-the-compression-moulding-process

18. Injection Molding Machine: Introduction & working Process, http://techminy.com/injection-molding-machine

19. Daniel Adams, "Choosing the most suitable methods for composites testing", Composites World, July 2017, https://www.compositesworld.com.

20. "Mechanical Testing of Composites", Quality Magazine, June 2014. https://www.qualitymag.com.

21. M. M. Yovanovich, "Micro and Macro Hardness Measurements, Correlations, and Contact Models", 44th AIAA Aerospace Sciences Meeting and Exhibit. Reno, Nevada, 2006.

22. ASTM D638 - 02a, Standard Test Method for Tensile Properties of Plastics," ASTM International, West Conshohocken, PA, 2002, www.astm.org

23. ASTM D7264 / D7264M-07, Standard Test Method for Flexural Properties of Polymer Matrix Composite Materials. Standard, West Conshohocken, PA: ASTM International, 2007, www.astm.org.

24. Pradeep V.Badiger, Rajesh G L, Vijaykumar Hiremath and Virupaxi Auradi, "Mechanical & Machining Characteristics of Al/B4C Metal Matrix Composites", http://www.academia.edu.

25. John Edward Wyatt, George J. Trmal, "Machinability: Employing a Drilling Experiment as a Teaching Tool", Journal of Industrial Technology, 22, 2006.

26. ASTM D5229 / D5229M-92, Standard Test Method for Moisture Absorption Properties and Equilibrium Conditioning of Polymer Matrix Composite Materials. Standard, West Conshohocken, PA: ASTM International, 1992, www.astm.org.

27. ASTM D570-98, Standard Test Method for Water Absorption of Plastics. Standard, ASTM International, West Conshohocken, PA, 1998, www.astm.org.

28. Iuliana IAŞNICU (STAMATE), Ovidiu VASILE, Radu IATAN, "Sound Absorption Analysis for Layered Composite", Proceedings of the Annual Symposium of the Institute of Solid Mechanics and Session of the Commission of Acoustics, Bucharest, 2015.

29. Stanciu, M. D., I. Curtu, Cosereanu C., D. Lica, and S. Nastac, "Research Regarding Acoustical Properties of Recycled Composites", 8th International DAAAM Baltic Conference, Tallinn, Estonia, 19-21 April 2012.

30. Küçük, Seçkin Çelebi and Haluk, "Acoustic Properties of Tea Leaf Fiber Mixed Polyurethane Composites", Cellular Polymers, 31, July 2012.

31. Eulalia Gliścińska, Marina Michalak, Izabella Krucińska, "Sound absorption property of nonwoven based composites", AUTEX Research Journal, 13, 150-155, December 2013.

32. M. D. Telia, A. Pal, Dipankar Roy, "Efficacy of nonwoven materials as sound insulator", Indian Journal of Fibre & Textile Research, 32, 202-206, 2007.

33. fibre2fashion, "Global nonwovens: Recent trends and future", http://www.fibre2fashion.com/industry-article.

34. Nazan Avcioglu Kalebek, Osman Babaarslan, "Fiber Selection for the Production of Nonwovens", Non-woven Fabrics, March 2016.

35. https://www.edana.org

36. Standard Catalogue, 2011, https://www.iso.org.

37. http://www.inda.org. about-nonwovens

38. M.J. Denton, P.N. Daniels, "Textile Terms and Definitions", 11th ed. The Textile Institute, Manchester, UK, 2002.

39. S.J. Russell, "Handbook of Nonwovens", Woodhead Publishing, Cambridge, UK, 2007.

40. Dipayan Das, S.M. Ishtiaque, Shivendra Yadav, "Evaluation of Fibre Orientation in Fibreweb", Indian Journal of Fibre & Textile Research, 39, 9-13, March 2014.

41. Vinay Kumar Midha, A Mukhopadyay, "Bulk and physical properties of needle-punched nonwoven fabrics", Indian Journal of Fibre & Textile Research, 30, 218-229, June 2005.

42. Han-Yong Jeon, Non-woven Fabrics, 2016

43. Dipayan Das and Behnam Pourdeyhimi, "Composite Nonwoven Materials Structure, Properties and Applications", Woodhead publication, Cambridge, UK, 2014.

44. Dipayan Das, Arun Kumar Pradhan, R. Chattopadhyay, S.N. Singh, "Nonwoven composite", Taylor & Francis, online, 2012.

45. Sunil Kumar Ramamoorthy, Mikael Skrifvars, "Nonwovens in composite industry for structural applications", Technical Textiles, http://www.technicaltextile.net.

46. G. S. Bhat, "Nonwovens as Three-Dimensional Textiles for Composites", Materials and Manufacturing Processes, 10, 667-688, 1995.

47. Mouritz A., Bannister M., Falzon P., Leong K, "Review of applications for advanced three-dimensional fibre textile composites", Composite Part A Applied Science and Manufacturing, 30, 1445–1461, December 1999.

48. Amit Rawal, Stepan Lomov, Thanh Ngo, Ignaas Verpoest and Jozef Vankerrebrouck, "Mechanical Behavior of Thru-air Bonded Nonwoven Structures", Textile Research Journal, 77, 417-431, June 2007.

49. M. Tausif, S.J. Russell, "Characterisation of the z-directional tensile strength of composite hydroentangled nonwovens", Polymer Testing, 31, 944-952, October 2012.

50. Amar Patnaik, Sachin Tejyan, "Mechanical and visco-elastic analysis of viscose fiber based needle punched nonwoven fabric mat reinforced polymer composites: Part I", Journal of Industrial Textiles, 43, 440–457, August 2012.

51. Hajnalka Hargitai, Ilona Rácz, Rajesh Anandjiwala, "Development of Hemp Fibre Reinforced Polypropylene Composite," Journal of Thermoplastic Composite Materials, February 2008.

52. Martin Nicolas, Davies Peter, Baley Christophe, "Evaluation of the potential of three non-woven flax fiber reinforcements: Spunlaced, needlepunched and paper process mats", Industrial Crops and Products, 83, 194-205, May 2016.

53. Josep Claramunt, Heura Ventura, Lucía J Fernández-Carrasco, Mònica Ardanuy, "Tensile and Flexural Properties of Cement Composites Reinforced with Flax Nonwoven Fabrics", Materials (Basel), 10(2), 215, February 2017.

54. A.H.M Fazle Elahi, Md. Milon Hossain, Shahida Afrin, Mubarak A. Khan, "Study on the Mechanical Properties of Glass Fiber Reinforced Polyester Composites", International Conference on Mechanical, Industrial and Energy Engineering, Khulna, Bangladesh, 26-27, December 2014.

55. H. Pakravan, M. Jamshidi, M. Latifi, and M. Neshastehriz, "Application of Polypropylene Nonwoven Fabrics for Cement Composites Reinforcement", Asian Journal of Civil Engineering (Building and Housing), 12, 551-562, 2011.

56. Muhammad Tausif, Achilles Pliakas, Tom O'Haire, Parikshit Goswami, and Stephen J. Russell, "Mechanical Properties of Nonwoven Reinforced Thermoplastic Polyurethane Composites", Materials (Basel) 10, Jun 2017.

57. J Žák, P Štemberk and J Vodička, "Production of a textile reinforced concrete protective layers with non-woven polypropylene fabric", IOP Conf. Series: Materials Science and Engineering, 246, 2017.

58. Pooja Katkar, C.A.Patil, Prakash Khude, A. M.Jain , S. S.Chougule, " Coir-cement composite", Melliand International, 18, 132-134, May 2012.

59. M. Award, S.M. Naga T. Khalifa, P. Greil and O. Russina, N.A. Ibrahim, "Fiber-Reinforced Alumina-Based Composites Using Nonwoven Cellulose Fabrics", American Ceramic Society Bulletin, April 2005.

60. Xiaoqun Zhang, "Investigation of Biodegradable Nonwoven Composites Based on Cotton, Bagasse & Other Natural Annual Plants", LSU Master's Theses, 2145, Tianjin University, Tianjin, August 2004, https://digitalcommons.lsu.edu/gradschool_theses/2145

61. M. G. Kamath, G. S. Bhat, D. V. Parikh, and D. Mueller, "Cotton Fiber Nonwovens for Automotive Composites", INJ Spring, 2005.

62. Eulalia Gliścińska1, Marina Michalak, Izabella Krucińska, Janusz Kazimierczak, Arkadiusz Bloda and Danuta Ciechańska, "Sound Absorbing Composites from Nonwoven and Cellulose Submicrofibres", J. Chem. Chem. Eng., 7, 942-948, October 2013.

63. S. Sakthivel, T. Ramachandran, Ms.G.Archana, Mr.Ezhilanban.J.J, Mr.V.M.S.Sivajith Kumar, "Sustainable Non-Woven Fabric Composites For Automotive Textiles Using Reclaimed Fibres", International Journal of Engineering Research and Development, 4, 11-13, November 2012.

64. Nazire Deniz Yilmaz, Nancy B. Powell, Pamela Banks-Lee, Stephen Michielsen, "Hemp-fiber Based Nonwoven Composites: Effects of Alkalization on Sound Absorption Performance", Fibers and Polymers, 13, 2012.

65. M.N. Satheesh Kumar, K.S. Manjula b, Siddaramaiah, "Transport behavior of n-alkane penetrants into castor oil based polyurethane–polyester nonwoven fabric composites", Journal of Hazardous Materials, 145, 36-44, June 2007.

66. M.N. Satheesh Kumar, Siddaramaiah, "Studies on Corn Starch Filled Poly (Styrene-Co-Butyl Acrylate) Latex Reinforced Polyester Nonwoven Fabric Composites", AUTEX Research Journal, 5, 228−235, December 2005.

67. Anita Grozdanov, Aleksandra Buzarovska, Maurizio Avella, Magdalena Prendjoval,Gennaro Gentile and Maria E. Errico, "Application of Non-

Woven Preforms Based on Natural Fibres as Reinforcement in Eco-Composites", http://www.escm.eu.org.

68. Maciej Jaroszewski, Janina Pospieszna, Jan Ziaja and Mariusz Ozimek, "Composites Made of Polypropylene Nonwoven Fabric with Plasmas Layers", Polypropylene by Fatih Dogan, 2012.

69. H.N. Dhakal, Z.Y. Zhang, M.O.W. Richardson, O.A.Z. Errajhi, "The low velocity impact response of non-woven hemp fibre reinforced unsaturated polyester composites", Composite Structures, 2006.

70. Yasuhide Shindo, Tomo Takeda, Fumio Narita, "Mechanical response of nonwoven polyester fabric/epoxy composites at cryogenic temperatures", Cryogenics, 52, 564-568, October 2012.

71. Henri Kröling, Johann Fleckenstein, Narmin Nubbo, Angelika Endres, Frank Miletzky & Ing. Samuel Schabel, "Non-Woven and Paper Based Epoxy Composites", 2014, www.ipwonline.

72. Mehmet Dasdemir, Benoit Maze, Nagendra Anantharamaiah, Behnam Pourdeyhimi, "Formation of novel thermoplastic composites using bicomponent nonwovens as a precursor", Journal of Mater Science., 46, 3269–3281, May 2011.

73. Rassmann, R.G. Reid, R. Paskaramoorthy, "Effects of processing conditions on the mechanical and water absorption properties of resin transfer moulded kenaf fibre reinforced polyester composite laminates", Composites Part A: Applied Science and Manufacturing, 41, 1612–1619, November 2010.

74. S. Rassmann, R. Paskaramoorthy, R.G. Reid, "Effect of Resin System on the Mechanical Properties and Water Absorption of Kenaf Fibre Reinforced Laminates", Materials & Design 32, 1399-1406, March 2011.

75. Youjiang Wang, "Effect of Consolidation Method on the Mechanical Properties of Nonwoven Fabric Reinforced Composites" Applied Composite Materials, 6, 19–34, 1999.

76. Rejaul Hasan, Rishad Rayyaan, "Effect of fibre geometry on the tensile properties of thermoset jute fibre composites", International Journal of Scientific and Research Publications, 4, October 2014.

77. Ayou Hao, Haifeng Zhao, Jonathan Y. Chen, "Kenaf/polypropylene nonwoven composites: The influence of manufacturing conditions on mechanical, thermal, and acoustical performance", Composites Part B: Engineering 54, 44-51, November 2013.

78. Sachin Tejyan, Vedant Singh, "Erosive Behavior of Polypropylene Fiber Based Needlepunched Nonwoven Reinforced Laminated Composites",

International Advanced Research Journal in Science, Engineering and Technology, 4, 14-17, February 2017.

79. Sengupta, Surajit, "Sound reduction by needle-punched nonwoven fabrics", Indian Journal of Fibre & Textile Research, 35, 237-242, 2010.

80. Nazan Avcioğlu Kalebek, "Sound Absorbing Polyester Recycled Nonwovens for the Automotive Industry", FIBRES & TEXTILES in Eastern Europe, 24, 107-113, 2016.

NOTES

ABOUT THE AUTHOR/S

Prof. (Dr.) P. V. Kadole:

Prof. (Dr.) P. V. Kadole is working as Director in DKTES Textile and Engineering Institute, Ichalkaranji. He has more than 30 years of experience in Yarn Manufacturing, Technical Textiles, Research, Product Development and Consultancy. He has published more than 100 papers in various national and international journals. He has guided more than eight PhD students. He has received various prestigious awards like Reiter award, Best Teacher award, Golden educationalist award, Life time education achievement award

Pooja Katkar:

Pooja Katkar is working as assistant professor in DKTES Textile and Engineering Institute, Ichalkaranji. She has more than 20 years of experience in field of textiles. She has published more than 40 papers in national and international journals. She is recipient of Innovative Work by Engineering College Teacher Award 2017 by ISTE.